CAMPANULAS
A GARDENER'S GUIDE

PETER LEWIS AND MARGARET LYNCH

BT Batsford Ltd London

Printed in Singapore

for the publishers
B.T. Batsford Ltd
583 Fulham Road
London
SW6 5BY

ISBN 0 7134 8266 4

A catalogue record for this book is available from the British Library

CONTENTS

Opposite: Campanula carpatica seedling at Wisley

Colour Plates

Figures

Roger Philippo

Introduction

Campanulas have an appeal for most plant lovers and there is a campanula to suit even the most selective gardener. The cottage gardener cannot do without them; the rock gardener looks on them as belonging to one of the few essential backbone genera; and the plantsman who loves a challenge for the alpine house or show bench can find material enough to keep him/her busy. Whether the gardener grows for the herbaceous border, for the alpine garden, bedding out or flower arranging, there is a bellflower which will suit and richly repay any time and effort given.

This book is a revision of one published by Christopher Helm some six years ago. Since that time, a number of new hybrids and cultivars have appeared, and some old names have changed. There is a continuing demand for information about campanulas, and with our original book out of print, it is time not just to reprint, but to revise where needed and republish with new photographs. There has been no overall treatment of the family since Crook's authoritative monograph some 40 years ago. It is now a rarity to be searched for in second-hand bookshops. Earlier accounts were either in the botanical literature or periodicals, and can only be found in specialist libraries.

In a genus of over 300 species, to which must be added many variants and hybrids, there is ample scope for a substantial volume. Further scientific research would be valuable to assemble the available information, and to sort out classification problems. Until this is done, the present book claims, as did our earlier edition, to describe the bellflowers that are available in cultivation, and to do this for the gardener and not the botanist.

We have also attempted to give some anecdotes of the history and discovery of various campanulas, as well as ideas on cultivation. In particular, we have tried to be fair and call a spade a spade – not all campanulas are good tempered or easy – although most of them are. We must again thank the following for their generous help, especially in the production of the first volume – the staff of the University of Cambridge Botanic Garden: Clive King, Peter Yeo, and the late Peter Orris. Mary Newnes and the late Will Ingwersen advised us too. Recent photographs have been taken, as well as in our own gardens, at Kiftsgate Court (Mr and Mrs J G Chambers), Bressingham Gardens (Jaime Blake), Hookwood Farmhouse (Mr and Mrs E Mason), and Rise Top Cottage (Trevor Bath). We are very grateful to the owners for their patience and help. A lot of

Campanula elatines var. elatinoides

effort and time was spent by photographer Howard Rice who provided many of the colour plates.

Thanks are also due to Blooms Photographic Library, and to Dr Chris Prior of RHS Plant Pathology at Wisley for information on rusts. We would like also to thank Richard Reynolds of Batsford for his patient guidance.

We have received many favourable and grateful comments on our first edition from plantsmen, gardeners and botanists, and we hope that this new edition will prove even more helpful to all who love the plants that we love.

A Brief History

hen, in *Cymbeline* Shakespeare extolled 'The azure bluebell like her veins' he was referring to what in England is called the Bluebell, *Scilla non-scripta*, an early spring bulb, and not a campanula. In Scotland, of course, the name bluebell is given to a campanula, *Campanula rotundifolia*, in England called the harebell. Whilst we concede that a great poet is at liberty to confuse a common name, it is regrettable that the confusion has commonly continued to this day – and, in fact, has increased, when we add the bluebells of Australia and New Zealand, which, although they are Wahlenbergias, are close relatives.

GERARD

Gerard, in his herbal of 1597, was one of the first to tackle the name of Campanula or Bellflowers. He describes 'Campanula medium' (now commonly called Canterbury Bells) thus:

'*Viola mariana*, Coventry Bells, which grow in woods, mountains and dark valleys and under hedges, especially about Coventry, where they grow plentifully abroad in the fields and are called Coventry Bells, and by some people about London Canterbury Bells, but improperly, for there is another kind of bellflower growing in Kent about Canterbury which may more fitly be called Canterbury Bells, because they grow there more plentifully than in any other countrey.'[1]

If it were not for his excellent description we would not be at all sure what plant Gerard was referring to. But he describes *Campanula medium* very clearly 'Coventry Bells have broad leaves, rough and hairy... among which do rise up stiffe hairy stalks the second year after the sowing of the seed, which stalks do divide themselves into sundry branches, whereupon grow many fair pleasant bellflowers... cut to the brim with five slight gashes... in the middle of the flowers be three or four whitish chives and also much downie hair such as in the eares of a dog or suchlike beast. So his Coventry Bell is our Canterbury Bell.'

Gerard then goes on to describe Throatwort or Coventry Bells. But here the Latin name gives us a clue, for he calls it *Trachelium majus*. It is our *Campanula trachelium*, a plant which we in England now call the Nettle-leaved Bellflower or Bats-in-the-Belfry, and which he called Canterbury Bells. This is, by the way, one of the few campanulas which the old herbalists thought had any medicinal use.

Campanula trachelium near Skiddaw, English Lake District

Gerard says 'We have found from our own experience that they are excellent good against the inflammation of the mouth and throat, to be gargled and washed with the decoction of them.'[1]

JOHN PARKINSON

John Parkinson, 'Paradisi in Sole' 1629, was also keen to check out Coventry. 'The Coventry Bells doe not grow wild in any of the parts about Coventry, as I am credibly informed by a faithful Apothecary dwelling there, called Master Brian Ball, but are noursed in gardens with them as they are in other places.'[2]

As *Medium* is not a British native this is clearly correct. Parkinson goes on to describe *Campanula persicifolia*, 'the peach-leaved Bellflowers white or blew', whose name has thankfully not changed from then till now. He gave a useful tip: 'The roote is very small, white and thready, creeping under the upper crust of the ground so that often times the heat and drought of the Summer will goe near to parch and wither it utterly; it requireth therefore to be planted in some shadowie place.'[2]

Good descriptions follow of *Campanula pyramidalis* which he calls 'The Great or Steeple Bellflower'. *C. medium* which he calls Coventry Bells, and *C. trachelium* which he calls Canterbury Bells. He illustrates and describes the double forms of *C. trachelium* which are so much sought after today. Plants which are probably *C. latifolia* and *C. glomerata* are given good descriptions as is the related *Lobelia cardinalis*.

The virtues of campanulas were not great, according to Parkinson. 'They may safely be used in gargles and lotions for the mouth, throate and other parts as occasion serveth. The roots of many of them, while they are young, are often eaten in sallets by divers beyond the seas.'[2]

CARL LINNAEUS

Carolus (Carl) Linnaeus took hold of campanula and set it in proper order, when he published his *Genera Plantarum* in 1737. He confirmed the name given to the genus by Fuchs, which has been followed ever since, as indeed has the rest of that account which was the start of modern systematic botany. He died, aged 70 in 1778, and at his funeral, 17 doctors of medicine, all his pupils, were pallbearers.

THE CAUCASUS AND GREECE

If campanulas have an epicentre it must be in the Caucasus, Eastern Europe, with Greece running as a close second. Distribution is discussed in the next chapter, but mention must be made of the lives of two very different men: Dr John Sibthorp, who gave his life to studying Greek flowers, and Marschall von Bieberstein, who lived in Russia and made his life's work Caucasian flowers. Sibthorp was born ten years earlier, but died when he was 38, while Bieberstein lived to be 58.

JOHN SIBTHORP

John Sibthorp was 25 in 1783 when he succeeded his father as Professor of Botany at Oxford. He was a very affluent young

Campanula versicolor in the garden

man, and arranged for a deputy to take over his job when three years later he went on his first botanical expedition. He took with him Ferdinand Bauer, a draughtsman, and travelled through the Mediterranean to Crete, then to Athens and Mount Olympus, and spent the winter in Constantinople. He visited 'the snowy heights of Parnassus, the steep precipices of Delphis, the empurpled mountain of Hymettus, the Pentele, the lower hills about the Piraeus, the olive grounds about Athens, and the fertile plains of Boetia'.[3]

He and Bauer sailed home from Patras in September with 2,000 specimens, about 300 of them new, and a large number of drawings. Sibthorp's health had not stood up well to the heat on the islands and the rough journey; but on this occasion he quickly recovered. Although he wished to return, pressure of work and politics kept him at home for seven years.

In 1794 he made another collecting trip. This started badly with a slow and stormy sea passage to Constantinople, where he arrived with a 'bilious fever and colic'.[4] But he went to Crete, climbed Mount Olympus, travelled to Troy and Mount Athos and back to Athens. He spent the winter on the Ionian island of Zante and from there, the next spring, visited the Peloponnese and climbed in the Teygetos mountains. His journeys were fraught with hazards. He lost a young colleague, Francesca Borone, who fell from a window in Athens while sleepwalking; had to dodge Barbary pirates; and then on the way home from Zante had another terrible sea voyage when bad weather prevented them from sailing for Italy. He arrived home with a fever and cough in the autumn of 1795, and died in Bath in 1796.

Sibthorp is credited in *Hortus Kewensis* 1810 with 14 introductions, including *Campanula versicolor*, a plant he found in the area of Mount Olympus. Rather like a small *Campanula pyramidalis*, its thick woody stem hangs from the rocks. *Campanula versicolor* took a long time to reach the gardening public for, in 1913, Farrer was saying it was 'still out of reach'.[5] The dramatic flower is bicoloured, light and dark blue, with a long projecting style.

Sibthorpe left £30,000 to pay for the publication, posthumously, of his superb ten-volume *Flora Graeca*, with Bauer's plates in 1806. Sir J. E. Smith, the editor, had no easy task, as Sibthorp's notes were often scanty: 'He trusted to his memory and dreamed not of dying.'[6]

BIEBERSTEIN

Friedrich August Marschall von Bieberstein, born in 1768, came to Russia from a military academy in Stuttgart. He joined the Russian army and served in the Crimea for three years. When he left in 1796, he joined an expedition of Count Zubov's to Persia, from where he explored the Western Caucasus. Two years later he explored the north and east of the range.

The first botanical work he wrote about this area, in French and German, was *Tableau des Provinces... entre les fleurs...* But much more important was *Flora Taurico-Caucasica* written in Latin in 1808, which covered 2,322 species, of which 17 were campanulas. These include *C. lactiflora*, which he introduced. He describes its favourite habitat as the Caucasian Alps, especially around the castle of Wladi-Kawkas on Mount Kaitchaur, where the campanula flowered in September.[7]

This flower is a sufficient monument for any botanist. It has all the virtues: tall, elegant and dripping with flowers. Bieberstein's *Flora* also included *Campanula adami* (now *tridentata*), which he may have named after a Dr. J. M. Adams who, with Bieberstein, was a botanical member of Count Massin-Puschkin's journey in the Caucasus. The expedition was quite unofficial, but the members sent seed and specimens, which were important introductions, back to Sir

Joseph Banks at Kew and to others. *Puschkinia scilloides* commemorates its leader.

Bieberstein went on no more organised collecting trips. But his new job, as inspector of silk-worm breeding, took him all over Southern Rusia from his home in Kharkov, and he had ample opportunity to look for Caucasian plants.

Dr F.E.L. von Fischer 1782–1854

FISCHER

Freidrich Ernst Ludwig von Fischer,
1782–1854, received a doctorate in his
native Germany. But he made his name as
the Director of the Imperial Botanic
Garden at St. Petersburg[8] laid out by Peter
the Great in 1714. In this post Dr. Fischer
travelled in England, France and Germany
in 1824 to purchase exotic plants, and he
returned with 2,320 species for the garden.
Dr. Anderson at Chelsea Physic Garden
received from him seed of *Campanula
latifolia* 'Macrantha' in 1825. He also sent
to Dr. Hunneman in England the seed of
Campanula sarmatica and *Campanula
speciosa*, which found its way to Kew.[8]

Dr Fischer gathered an enormous
private herbarium of 60,000 species. His
most important work was a catalogue of
the plants in the Imperial Garden which
listed many new species. In it, for instance,
he mentions *Campanula grandis* (now *C.
latiloba* or *C. persicifolia* subspecies
sessiliflora), a fine garden plan. He
mentions *C. glomerata* var. *dahurica*, which
is one of the best *C. glomerata* varieties.
Sadly we have no description or note of
where it was collected, although Dahurica
lies in the area of Lake Baykal in Siberia.
Many of his herbarium specimens were
inadequately labelled and did not give
exact locations of the plants collected, just
saying, for instance, 'China'.[9]

In 1850 he was compelled to leave his
post owing to irregularities in the accounts,
and he died four years later. His herbarium
was bought from his widow by Imperial
order for 1,000 roubles.[9]

OTHER NOTABLE RUSSIANS

It is possible that there are more exciting
campanulas still flowering unseen in the
Caucasus; perhaps with increasing access
they will be found. A novelty of just the
rare and intractable sort that gardeners love
was discovered in 1894: *Campanula
mirabilis*.

Nicholas Michaelovich Albov was on
his second journey to the Caucasus He
spotted a plant growing in a rock fissure
91m (300ft) above his path, and sent a
guide to dig it out. It was the only plant;
thorough examination of the
neighbourhood revealed no more. When
the parcel containing it finally turned up at
the Boissier herbarium in Switzerland it
was examined minutely but, though it had
100 flowers, there was no seed. A further
desperate examination revealed a single
capsule, and in it ripe seed.[10] From that, all
the stock in Europe was eventually raised.

At Kew it caused a sensation when it
formed a pyramid of 300 flowers in 1899:
everyone wanted it. But the Rev. Wolley
Dod, a practical man, was the first to say
that he could not get it to flower. It is
monocarpic and difficult, sometimes taking
six years to reach flowering size.

THE MOUNTAINS OF EUROPE
ALPHONSE DE CANDOLLE

Gardeners and botanists alike were excited
by the exotic new plants being brought
from the Orient. Nearer home, the
European Alps had been thoroughly
explored by the 19th century, and their
campanulas recorded. So the time was right

in 1830 for the first monograph on the genus, written in Geneva by Alphonse de Candolle.[11]

He was born in Paris in 1806. His father Augustin was Professor of Botany at Geneva. At his father's insistence, Alphonse took a law degree, but he never practised; instead, he took over his father's great work, the *Prodromus*[12], and continued it, writing up 26 of the families himself, though he never finished the work. The dynasty continued with his son Casimir.

Edmund Boissier 1810–1885

EDMOND BOISSIER

Another great researcher was compiling his magnum opus in Geneva at the same time. This was Edmond Boissier. He was a systematic botanist who had travelled in Asia Minor in 1842 and published descriptions of the new species he found on his journeys. This paved the way for his elaborate *Flora Orientalis* in five octavo volumes which was completed in 1881. It covered a huge area, and was based on his own collection and that of other botanical travellers.

Boissier was that unusual species, a gardening botanist. He grew a large collection of alpines at his home at Valeyres near Geneva. With his friend Henri Correvon, he was one of the founders of the Society for the Protection of Alpine Plants.[13]

CORREVON

Henri Correvon, 1854–1939, was a more modern man. He was a conservationist who had seen 'Peasants of Savoy or Valais bringing baskest full of uncommon species for sale at Geneva market as classical sites were already becoming exhausted.[14]

He wrote from his own experience a description of the campanulas he saw

Henri Correvon 1854–1939

which was serialised in *The Garden* in 1901. It was intended for gardeners, and is full of practical hints and personal observation: 'It is a fact that nowhere in the world are the campanulas grown and appreciated as much as in England.'[15]

He also recognised one of the problems that would be faced by keen amateurs wanting to grow the alpine species. 'The campanulas, being for the most part plants of a strong and healthy constitution, easily adapt themselves to new conditions... in this way they lose their hairy surface, relax their tissues, increase the size of their leaves and add to the number of their flowers, while contracting their corollas, so that some species become almost unrecognisable. To such a degree is this the case that one day when visiting Miss Willmott's rich collection at Warley, I found it difficult to recognise certain species of campanula, the actual plants of which had come from my own garden.'[15]

There now started a new fashion for campanulas. The 19th century had been a rich period for plant introductions; in the 20th, eminent horticulturalists took up the work.

PRICHARD

Maurice Prichard wrote a lavishly illustrated account of campanulas in the *RHS Journal* in 1902.

'Perhaps no family of hardy plant is more generally admired than the Bellflowers or Campanulas, presumably on account of the elegance and informality of their growth, and wonderful freedom of flowering.'[16]

He did a fair amount of plant breeding at his Riverslea nursery: *Campanula carpatica* 'White Star' which received its Award of Merit in 1905, is still vigorous today. Between 1929 and 1931 six other *Campanula carpatica* cultivars were submitted to the RHS and received Awards of Merit. In 1935 *C. grandis* 'Highcliffe' received its AM after being sent in by Prichard: 'It is still the strongest variety.'

And there were many more.

BEDDOME

By the early 19th century the names of many campanulas had attracted a great many synonyms. So in 1907 a retired Indian Army Colonel, Richard Henry Beddome, published an 'Annotated List of the Species of Campanula' in the *RHS Journal*. This was intended to sort out many problems for the amateur nurserymens' catalogues... '[the names] are often very puzzling, so that amateurs wishing to form a good collection are often frustrated, and buy the same plant over and over again under different names.'[17]

FARRER

Reginald Farrer gave his usual emphatic and salty comments on campanulas in *The English Rock Garden*, published in 1918. '*Campanula barbata* is the noble bearded bell of the Alps, and one of their most lovely glories, when its stout campanili of fluffy china-blue wave amid golden arnica in the showering grasses.'[18]

Reginald Farrer

'*Campanula petraea* is a species of great rarity and great ugliness, from the rocks of Tyrol... It is not a biennial, but the gardener sometimes wishes it were, the plant's rarity otherwise protecting it from removal by any irreverent hand.'[18]

But, for all his jokes, he took campanula very seriously, and his account also wrestled with the synonyms and muddled classification: 'This august race is so vast and so complicated that the best thing is to plunge into it at once and go through its serried ranks with care seeing the huge confusion that there reigns and the necessity of weeding the many beautiful sheep from the many goats in the family.'[20]

CROOK

The modern work on campanulas was published in 1951 by H. Clifford Crook:

Campanulas, their cultivation and classification. The fact that there was an interval of 121 years between it and the previous monograph indicates the size of the task of classification which Clifford Crook undertook: it took him 30 years and extensive travel. He illustrated it with his own black-and-white photographs, mostly taken in the wild, of 216 of the 300 or so species.

This is still the standard work, quoted by both gardeners and botanists, and it is likely to remain so at the moment – though, sadly, it is out of print. Clifford Crook admired the Greek mountain campanulas, and in 1940 he showed *C. oreadum* at the RHS. He received an AM for this delightful subject for the alpine house, with its hairy grey leaves, fragile stems and large narrow bells.

BAILEY

Campanulas are not, in the main, a North American genus, but they had their champion in the United States in Dr. Liberty Hyde Bailey, who wrote his *Garden of Bellflowers in North America* in 1953. It was intended as a horticultural account of the plants which were than available to growers in the US. His account is straightforward, and written from a garden 'fully inhabited by Bellflowers'[21] in preparation for the book. 'Perhaps one reason why I have been attracted to the Bellflowers from my youth is because they are not hopelessly confused by hybridisation. There is now a persistent effort to cross everything that is crossable until original lines of singularity are lost, and the natural and distinctive marks of separation have no meaning... The best gardener is also the best naturalist.'[21]

INGWERSEN

The name Ingwersen is linked to the fortunes of some very good campanulas. Walter Ingwersen introduced *C. poscharskyana* in 1933 which devours space, covering walls and poor soil with its simple, star-shaped blue flowers. He has in fact been quoted as saying it is one of the few plants he felt some regrets about having introduced into cultivation.

C. poscharskyana is nonetheless grown and enjoyed by gardeners across the world who make use of its flowery rampageous temperament. His son Will had an answer: 'Feed the stems and leaves to your children's pet rabbits, if they are short of greens – they appear to prefer it to anything else.'[23]

Will Ingwersen VMH, introduced *Campanula rotundifolia* 'Olympica' from Washington State, USA, with larger, deep violet bells than the type (AM 1931). The family nursery is famous for its alpines, and they put forward many good species of campanula to the RHS in London. Awards of Merit have been given to *C. laciniata* in 1945, *C. atlantis* in 1952, 'Birch Hybrid' 1945, *C. hercegovina* 'Nana' in 1946 and *C. ephesia* in 1956. They have sold and popularised many of the difficult alpine campanulas, but Will Ingwersen returns again and again in his writings to a simple one – *Campanula portenschlagiana*.

Liberty Hyde Bailey

'One of the best known and most deservedly popular of all campanulas must be *C. portenschlagiana*. There never was a better plant than this. A measure of its popularity is that, although I find it listed in a catalogue of alpine plants issued in 1903, and that it is to be seen in almost any garden, it remains a bestseller and is in constant and unfailing demand.'[24]

BLOOM

Herbaceous campanulas excited Alan Bloom's attention when he was breeding many herbaceous plants at Bressingham in Norfolk in the 1960s. Dwarf varieties of some hardy but tall stalwarts were one answer to the task of staking, and they looked good in the island beds which he popularised. In 1963 *Campanula glomerata*

'Purple Pixie' receved a PC from the RHS. The deep blue and sturdy *C. lactiflora* 'Prichard's Variety' was exhibited by Alan Bloom in 1964, and was given an AM. Two years later the well-named *C. lactiflora* 'Pouffe' received an AM, and made the wonderful *C. lactiflora* flowers available for the small garden. Alan Bloom also received an AM for *Campanula carpatica* 'Bressingham White' in 1967.

Ever the plantsman, Alan Bloom can always be relied on to spot a good plant. We have him to thank for the re-introduction of *C. trachelium* 'Bernice', which is double lavender-blue. This could even be the same plant described by Parkinson in 1629, which he received from 'friends beyond the seas'.[2] Giving nothing away, Alan Bloom also reported that he received his stock from abroad.

A few interesting, beautiful and popular plants have appeared since the above was written for the first edition. Among these it may not be out of place to mention *Campanula takesimana*, its selected form of 'Elizabeth', and also the hybrid 'Kent Belle', both from the nursery of Elizabeth Strangman in Sussex, and the fruit of her observant eye.

References

1. J. Gerard, *The Herbal or General Historie of Plants* (1597) p.448
2. J. Parkinson, *Paradisi in Sole* (1629) p.354
3. J. E. Smith, *Rees' Cyclopedia* (1819–20), under Sibthorp
4. A. Coats, *The Quest for Plants* (1969) p.26
5. R. Farrer, *The English Rock Garden* (1918), p.205
6. J. E. Smith, *Letters*, quoted in Coats
7. F. A. Marschall von Bieberstein, *Flora Taurico-Caucasica* (1808-1819)
8. *Curtis Botanical Magazine*, 2019
9. Bretschneider, *Botanical Discoveries* (1898), p.319
10. H. Correvon, 'The Genus Campanula' *The Garden* (Aug. 1901), p.112
11. Alphonse de Candolle, *Monographie des Campanulées* (1830)
12. Augustin and Alphonse de Candolle *Prodromus Systematis Naturalis* (1824–1873)
13. *Gardeners' Chronicle* (Oct 1885), p.455
14. H. Correvon and P. Robert, *The Swiss Alpine Flora*, English Translation (1911), p.23
15. *The Garden* (June 1901), p.451
16. M. Prichard, 'The Genus Campanula' *RHS Journal* (1902), p.98
17. Col. R. H. Beddome, 'An Annotated List of the Species of Campanula' *RHS Journal* (1907), p.196
18. Farrer, *English Rock Garden* (1918), p.162
19. Ibid., p.187
20. Ibid., p.157
21. L. H. Bailey, *Garden of Bellflowers in North America* (1953), pp.1, 2
22. *Gardeners' Chronicle* (Feb. 1972), p.35
23. Ibid., (Aug. 1976), p.41
24. Ibid., (1966), p.353

Classification and General Characteristics

Campanula is the type genus of Campanulaceae, the Bellflowers, a family which also includes the relatively familiar garden plant genera of *Adenophora*, *Codonopsis*, *Edraianthus*, *Platycodon*, *Trachelium* and *Wahlenbergia*. Somewhat less well known, perhaps, are *Asyneuma*, *Cyananthus*, *Jasione* (well known in the wild by alpine plantsmen), *Michauxia*, *Phyteuma*, and *Ostrowskia*. *Lobelia* is also closely related, though the irregular arrangement of the corolla here moves it to a separate sub-family, *Lobelioidae*, in most modern classifications.

With something in the order of 300 species, campanulas are found exclusively in the northern hemisphere, with their epicentre in the Mediterranean lands, particularly Greece and Turkey and their islands, and in the Caucasus. They are strongly represented in the Balkans, and tendrils stretch through southern Europe, through Spain into North Africa, where the Atlas Mountains in particular harbour a number of species. Further arms stretch though western to northern Europe, including the British Isles, to which about half a dozen are probably native, and through central Europe to Siberia. The Himalayas reveal a miscellany of small, closely related Bellflowers which, apart from *C. cashmeriana*, are hardly garden-worthy. Several quite well known campanulas find their homes in Japan, in Kamchatka, and in the islands, including the Aleutians, stretching up and over into North America, where the genus is not strongly represented, but, if anything, more commonly so in the west of that Continent.

On a global scale the campanula most commonly found in the wild is the native British 'Harebell' (in Scotland the 'Bluebell') which, together with its 30-odd close relatives (if you agree with the 'splitters'!), is found throughout the temperate and subarctic regions of the northern hemisphere, in Europe, Asia and North America. To the gardener this is *Campanula rotundifolia*, the name under which a host of similar plants will be treated in this publication, special mention being made only of the more outstanding 'forms', such as *C. linifolia* 'Covadonga' (a specific name which, alas, has also recently undergone revision).

The flowers of campanula are regular and bisexual, and their parts are normally in fives. The corolla is made up of five petals fused at the base, where the five stamens, though free from it and from each other, are inserted. This is perhaps the place to make a passing reference to the symphyandras, which in general only differ from campanulas in that their stamens are joined at the base, forming a tube. This feature is complicated by the fact that in some campanulas the stamens can also be partly fused, at least in the immature flower, to the point that some botanists have commented that there is little justification other than tradition for keeping the two separated. This said, we admit that we have not included symphyandras here.

The style, which connects the ovary to the stigma, is most often divided into three. In some species it is divided in five, but in each case the ovary has the equivalent number of chambers. The ovary is always inferior in campanula: that is to say, it is a swelling in the part of the flower stem below the insertion of the petals and sepals. The seed capsule, again a characteristic of the family, splits by pores when the seed is ripe. The pores may lie at the base or at the apex; in either case, the ripened capsule is held so that the pores are at the higher end, and thus seed only tends to be shed when wind shakes the capsule. This simple device ensures, as far as is possible, that seed is carried at least some distance from the plant. In many species the seed is very fine, and can in fact be carried farther than one would anticipate.

The calyx, the five green leaf-like sepals below the petals, surrounds the ovary. The shape of these lobes, and the existence or absence of further appendages between them, are useful diagnostic features for identifying plants. We make no apology for labouring these features for the gardener who wishes to be sure of his/her plants.

Apart from *Campanula vidalii*, more correctly known as *Azorina vidalii* which is shrubby, all campanulas are herbaceous, most tending to die back to underground rhizomes or carrot-like taproots, in winter. The stems bear alternate leaves without small leaflets, stipules, at their base. A strong family characteristic, which associates the family fairly closely with the daisy family, *Compositae (Asteraceae)*, is the presence in the tissues of the milky sap, inulin - a virtue which, although it may protect the plant from the ubiquitous goat to a certain extent, does little enough to protect it from the even more ubiquitous snail and slug, as the gardener soon learns to his cost. In the temperate zone garden, flowers are most likely to be pollinated by honey and other bees, especially bumblebees, and, to a lesser extent, hoverflies. Butterflies and moths show no interest.

A most interesting feature of campanulas, and this time one more valuable to the gardener, is the pollination method. The anthers ripen within the flower while it is as yet an unopened bud. They shed pollen on to the hairs borne on the style which only becomes ripe for fertilisation after the opening of the flower. Then its stigmas become receptive to pollen carried by bees seeking nectar in the disc at the base of the flower. In most cases this cross-pollination by insects will be successful, but there is an additional insurance mechanism in the unsuccessful case; here the stigmas gradually curl over

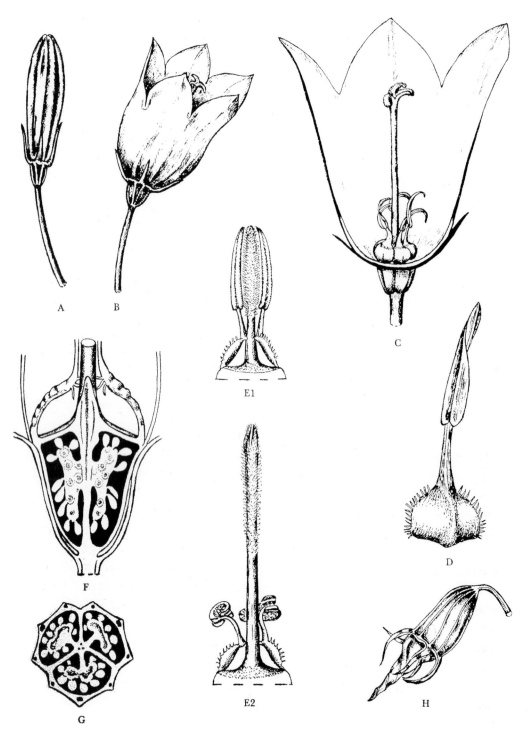

Campanula rotundifolia: the floral structure – see right

A A flower-bud, showing the corolla surrounded by the five linear lobes of the calyx. The ribbed calyx-tube is adnate to the inferior ovary. Bud: 12 x 3mm.

B the regular, bisexual flower at anthesis, shown as erect though it is nodding on the plant. The campanulate corolla has five lobes that are shorter than the tube. Corolla: 14 x 13mm. Calyx-lobe: 5mm

C L.S. of flower, showing the stamens and style. The five stamens alternate with the five corolla-lobes and the expanded bases of the filaments form a dome over the nectar-secreting disc at the base of the style. The anthers have shrivelled and the three branches of the style have begun to separate in order to expose the stigmatic surface.

D A complete stamen. The anther is introrse, two-celled and dehisces longitudinally. It is attached by its base to a short filament which is considerably enlarged at the base and edged with hairs.

E The reproductive organs in the male and female stages.

E1 The style and two of the five stamens as they appear inside the flower-bud. At this stage, the style is only as long as the stamens and the anthers are able to deposit their pollen on to the hairy upper part of the style.

Filament: 2.5mm   Anther: 5mm   Style + stigma: 7.5mm

E2 The style and 2 of the stamens at early anthesis. The style has lengthened, extending its pollen-covered portion well beyond the stamens. The stamens have begun to wither after shedding their pollen. (See C for next stage of style development.) Style + stigma: 10 mm

F L.S. of the inferior ovary. Numerous anatropous ovules are borne on axile placentas. Above the ovary is the nectar-secreting disc, protected by the expanded bases of the filaments. Loculus of ovary: 2 x 0.5mm

G T.S. of ovary formed from three united carpels, showing the three loculi with numerous ovules in each. Ovary: 1.75mm in diameter

H The fruit before dehiscence. The withered corolla and calyx enclose a subglobose capsule which opens by basal pores. Capsule: 5 x 2.5mm

---

and down until their adhesive tips will pick up pollen from their own style where it was left by the now withered stamens. This fail-safe mechanism greatly increases the chance of successful fertilisation and consequent seed formation.

From the cultivator's point of view, this method of fertilisation generally means an abundance of seed set. In those species where there would seem to be a measure of self-sterility – this applies particularly to the high alpines – there is still usually a small amount of viable seed to be obtained, albeit with much patience, good eyesight and agile fingers.

Hybrids are known, though rare in nature; in cultivation they are not as numerous as the size of the genus would suggest. In practice the principal perpetrators are few: *Cc. carpatica, cochlearifolia* and *rotundifolia*, and, to a lesser extent, *Cc. isophylla, punctata* and *pyramidalis*, but even here the hybrids will not often be met, even by those who grow a wide selection together. Incidentally, a notable exception is the inevitable crossing of *Campanula raineri* with *C. carpatica* whenever the latter gets a chance of quiet bee-assisted promiscuity. However, the species mentioned give rise to some of the most popular cultivars, propagation of which is, of course, confined to vegetative means.

The prevailing colour of the bellflowers,

it is hardly needful to say, is blue: from a deep violet to the very palest milky blue. White variants occur frequently. There is a red element in the inheritance which, in some species and a few notable cultivars, shows itself in soft pink colorations. One or two species reveal a yellow inclination, but except for the tender annual, *C. sulphurea*, an attractive sulphur-yellow little plant from the Middle East, the yellow manifests itself as a rather shabby-looking straw shade. This applies to the commonest of this colour, *C. thyrsoides*, which is perhaps more interesting than beautiful; though its subspecies, *carniolica*, can be really yellow.

In the genus are annuals, biennials, monocarpics and perennials, which can be both long or short-lived. In general the annuals are not a very interesting lot, and, almost without exception are not met with in cultivation. This is neither surprising nor likely to change. The biennials include, of course, the Canterbury Bell, which has now rather fallen out of favour for no detectable reason except the vagaries of fashion. The monocarpic campanulas – that is, those that may last several years before flowering, after which they die – are numerous, especially those from the Mediterranean region. Most of these are much hardier than is generally realised, and for bonuses have a decorative leaf-rosettes while maturing, and usually leave copious seed for propagation purposes. The perennials form the backbone of the cultivated species, showing a remarkable range of forms, dimensions and degrees of difficulty

– or ease – in cultivation.

Campanulas vary in size from ground-hugging alpines barely 25mm (one inch) high, rambling attractively over the rocks or scree in which they grow, to majestic pyramids 2m (6ft) or more in height which rival their illustrious cousin *Ostrowskia magnifica*, a superb but difficult plant which is rarely seen in gardens.

As one expects of any family, botanical, zoological – or human! – certain characters and tendencies crop up repeatedly to a greater or lesser extent. Roots, whether rhizomes or taproots, tend to be woody, thick and coarse. Basal leaves frequently wither near or at flowering, and tend to be on fairly long stalks; stem leaves are on shorter ones or completely stalkless. Most leaves are either oval, heart-shaped or lance-shaped in varying degrees; many are notched or toothed.

The family has another characteristic, which can be very confusing. The plants' size and outline vary considerably depending on where they are grown. The mountain plants especially will be much larger and floppier in soft lowland conditions. A number of writers have commented on this, and said that sometimes a plant can be unrecognisable at first glance. Such features as leaf-size, length of stalk, flower size, pendent or upright habit, are all variable as conditions change. It cannot be over-emphasised that most of the commonly grown species are extremely variable in appearance, which includes size and shade of flower, shape of leaf, etc. It should be noted that basal- and stem-leaf shapes are usually different, and that, typically, the former wither at anthesis – the time of flowering.

The botanical features of the flower have been summarised, and, apart from the feature of their petals being fused at the base, the flower presents as a bell, a trumpet, or as a star also – *vide C. carpatica* – as a salver or saucer. In the garden flowers may be doubled in the most popular cultivars, when they can present as cup-and-saucer, cup-in-cup or as multiples to rival the cabbage rose. Such doubles usually demand more care for them to give of their best.

Campanulas are high-summer flowering plants, essential ingredients of the summer border, and, indeed, of the rock garden. One has only to read William Robinson, Gertrude Jekyll and Reginald Farrer to realise that the garden would be immeasurably poorer without them even when they are not consciously given pride of place.

We should end this part with emphasis on the fact that we have made no pretence at any sort of a botanical classification, for which we are not in any case competent. Several – De Candolle in his *Monographie des Campanulées*, Damboldt in the *Flora of Turkey* and Fedorov in the *Flora of the USSR* – works for which we have the greatest respect, and to which we have constantly referred, have in their way endeavoured to give a structure to the genus and to inter-relate the species. Apart from the first, which dates from 1830, and which is incomplete, the others only treat

restricted areas, albeit the most important for campanulas, and must by definition also be incomplete. The groupings, be they subgenera, sections, subsections or other artificial arrangements, are only of occasional and limited practical use to the gardener or plantsman. We have therefore ignored them. Even when genetic methods have systematised the genus, their conclusions are not likely to help the cultivator very often, although, incidentally, we are given to understand by the work already done by such methods that there is little to improve on the conclusions of De Candolle 165 years ago! By the same token we have ignored the occasional criticism of the first edition that we have included no identification keys. There are three reasons for this omission: firstly, no key would be of great value unless it included all 300-odd species, together with their subspecies, varieties and cultivars, making such an immensely clumsy work. Secondly, such a key would guarantee that the book would not be used by gardeners! The third (and main) reason, if another is wanted, is that the book would scarcely be ready, from our hands, for another half-century while we got it made up, tried and proved. In contemporary terms, it is not our thing. We know that those to whom this volume is addressed will understand each of these reasons. To those who do not we tender our sincere apologies, for we would dearly like to be capable of producing such a key for our own use.

CULTIVATION, PROPAGATION, PESTS AND DISEASES

CULTIVATION OF BORDER PLANTS

The cultivation of campanulas usually grown in the open border presents no particular difficulties; they have no strong likes or dislikes, and will tolerate most reasonable garden conditions. To have them give of their best, however, the sensitive gardener (is this what 'green-fingers' is about?) will realise that just as gardeners, like anyone else, do their best when they are free to express their own preference, so will their plants when the same rule of (green) thumb applies. The cultivation of the more challenging alpine species can be a different story, which will be dealt with as they occur.

Campanulas prefer sun for at least part of the day, and some for most or all of it. They will, however, tolerate quite heavy shade if inevitable. Lime in the soil is a frequent preference except in the case of a small minority – which do not concern us here. A well-drained soil is essential; a low-lying spot which is waterlogged in winter for any length of time is guaranteed to rot or freeze taproot or rhizome beyond recovery. No doubt this applies to most garden plants other than bog plants.

Many campanulas grow on quite impoverished soil in nature, and in habitats where competition from other plants - especially grasses – is strong. Although in such circumstances they give a good account of themselves, they are never of the stature or floriferousness we look for in the garden, and of which they are more than capable. Examples are C. *persicifolia* as it grows in the high country meadows of the Pyrenees, where it is hard put to grow to 30cm (one foot), and bears but a few flowers on its meagre stem; and C. *glomerata* on the thin soils of the South Downs of England, where the 'cluster' of the Clustered Bellflower is a poor sight. In his highly respected monograph Clifford Crook depicted the former in the wild, and it is scarcely recognisable.

Many of the campanulas are great travellers! A few need to be watched on this account, especially if the soil is sandy or peaty; not many are positively menacing, and it is little trouble to deal with them as necessary, but they do reveal a liking for new ground. An occasional lifting, dividing of the rootstock and replanting will reinvigorate even the most fatigued stay-at-home.

Campanula glomerata in the wild, height 3cm

If there be a 'florist's' flower in the genus, it is *C. persicifolia*. This reacts well to being moved on every year or two. The more finicky doubles like to be moved annually, and require feeding in addition. For most of the border bellflowers a yearly sprinkle of bonemeal pricked into the surface of the soil will amply suffice. An autumn mulch is helpful. When these hungrier species are cultivated in containers, they will need regular feeding, especially in spring and when re-establishing after flowering, at which time they should be cut back to the basal leaves.

After flowering the stems may also be cut back to prevent indiscriminately self-sown seedlings arising when a modest second flowering may result; or seed may be saved - it is usually copious. If it is to be saved, the warning of the late Will Ingwersen is worth recalling: 'Many a watch has been kept at the front door while the seed has slipped out of the back unnoticed.' Timing is the watchword.

CULTIVATION OF ALPINE PLANTS

The genus is essentially one from the mountains and high places of the northern hemisphere. There are many species, therefore, that fall into the category 'alpine and rock garden plants'. There are long lists in catalogues and their diversity is great, from both the botanist's and the gardener's point of view. As we are unashamedly adopting the latter, the scope is somewhat diminished, and may be divided into three categories:

- alpines for any and every garden
- those for the specialist rock-gardener
- those which the most experienced plantsmen find a challenge to grow well and to keep.

Of these three categories, this account concerns itself principally with the first, though we hope that growers of the other two may also find help. This is not a comprehensive account of the genus, which must await another occasion. In numerous cases, species may be grouped, a precedent set by writers such as Crook and Farrer. For example, we deal with *C. rotundifolia*, the common harebell or bluebell, as a group, even though *Flora Europaea* may break it up into some 25 species, without counting those which could be added from North America and the vast stretches of Asia. It is certain, anyway, that those which have been in cultivation for any length of time will have cross-fertilised, and so lost any distinctive characters which may, in the eyes of a botanist somewhere, have justified specific status. The observant and enthusiastic gardener or plantsman will be content to note the plant as 'a good form' in colour, habit or length of flowering, and worth propagating vegetatively in order to keep it and to share it.

In dealing with the alpines, we have selected species and cultivars obtainable in commerce. They may not, it is true, be found on the 'alpines' display of every garden centre. They can be looked for either as seeds or plants in the lists of specialist nurseries. Seed is also offered to their members by several of the specialist plant societies (see p. 170) - the campanula list is often among the longest. The plants may also be found at the sales tables of their meetings and shows. Remember, though, that this is a bit of a lucky dip. The name will only be as accurate as the records of the member who collected and sent it in.

The special needs of each species are mentioned in the following descriptions, but a few general comments may not be out of place.

It has been said that the three rules for success in growing alpine plants are: drainage; drainage and drainage. Whether this is a matter of water drainage or porosity to oxygen remains an unsettled question, but it is probably both; a gritty, porous but not necessarily impoverished soil is certainly beneficial. The ideal – largely unattainable to most of us, but still to be striven for – is a good loam with sand and grit in it. As an indicator, we use a John Innes-type compost[1] with up to an equal volume of 50:50 sharp sand and 6mm (¼ in) grit, for pot work and for propagation, and as a standard to aim at in the open ground. This said, it must also be emphasised that most campanulas are accommodating and easy of cultivation.

Many bellflowers are of creeping habit and a few even troublesome in this respect. Indeed, such species owe their success in nature to this characteristic, witness C. *rapunculoides*, among the more rampageous. It has been suggested from garden evidence that these species seem to exhaust the soil of some essential nutrient; they do not sicken it, nor are other genera in any way impeded subsequently. Unfortunately, investigation, chemical or otherwise, is not likely to be undertaken, as it would doubtless be very costly and nobody would stand to make a fortune out of it! In practice, trespassing campanulas are not a great problem, and as a rule of thumb it may be said that the part which spreads is the part to take for propagation. Skill with a hoe can handle most problems!

Alpine campanulas like an open sunny aspect. Once well established they can take considerable drought, and prolonged frost and cold will not harm them; their good humour under these two stresses depends upon a good root-system. It must be added that many are completely deciduous, dying back so completely in winter that many have inadvertently suffered at the hoe or trowel of enthusiastic gardeners of the tidying-up strain. If it is worth keeping, it is worth marking; with a label that the birds will not scatter around the bed. If seed is not wanted, many small campanulas, like their larger sisters, may be given a haircut, when they will flower again, albeit less freely.

PROPAGATION

There is not a wide selection of seed of campanula species available commercially, and the chief source must be the seed exchanges of the specialist societies; over the past few years nearly 250 variants of Campanula have been offered. It is possible to recover more than the cost of the annual subscription of such societies on the value of the seed alone, without taking into account other benefits, including the expertise of other growers shared in their periodicals. Addresses of these societies may be found on p. 170. The source of such seed is, of course, the private grower; an incentive to collect from one's own plants.

Campanula species are easily grown from seed. This may be sown in late winter or early spring in trays or pots of good compost; a John Innes based compost[1] is considered best, with the addition of half the volume of extra grit. The seed should be sown thinly on the surface, and covered with only the finest layer of sharp sand or fine grit. This will discourage liverworts, but it should be thin, as light is beneficial to germination; trays should not be covered with paper etc. As the seed is often very fine, watering is best done by soaking the tray in water before standing out. Frost will not harm the seeds, even those growing toward the southern end of their natural range, and may well hasten germination by breaking dormancy, but the tray should, of course, be sheltered from heavy rain, wind and birds: a cold frame is hard to better. After germination the seedlings may be brought into a warmer spot to be kept moving, and pricking out should be done when they are quite small, with four or so true leaves, so they will quickly establish; but no harm will be done if this is delayed. They can be potted on if necessary, and then planted out when the soil has had the opportunity to warm up and a strong-growing rosette has been formed. Any

special treatment will be given under the individual species.

There are those who prefer, or find it more convenient to use, soil-less composts. Germination and early development of the seedling in this case may be very good, but we find that problems tend to start when it is desired to wean plants so started into open ground. The lush top growth makes an attractive-looking plant, but the soft root growth receives something of a shock when it has to tackle the rigours of a garden loam, however well tilled; hence the advice given in the past with many commercial plants to mix an abundance of peat in with the soil into which the plant is being set. In our opinion a soil-grown plant is more able to adapt and, in the long run, is quicker to establish. The reader may conclude that this is a matter of prejudice, but it is one built on personal experience. However, 'the devil you know...': the properties of which, best known to the individual grower, are most likely to give best results.

We have mentioned that frost access to the seed-tray will be beneficial; this applies to the vast majority of campanulas, including the Greek and Turkish ones, and many from the Mediterranean. When seed arrives too late in the year to catch frosts, as so often it does, it may be mixed with a small amount of moistened, very fine sand, and placed in a polythene bag in a refrigerator for a few weeks as artificial vernalisation; but particular care needs to be taken with the finer seed, lest the eventual sowing be too deeply covered.

We have found that campanula seed, placed in a well-sealed plastic box with a little silica gel to keep it dry, will remain viable in a refrigerator for a number of years, and we make a regular practice of storing in this manner.

Division of established plants, where possible, is best undertaken in the spring when new growth is getting going. Clumps can be divided quite drastically, when any piece with a root or vestige of root may be placed in a gritty compost until it is well rooted, and then planted out as desired. Additional feeding, except in the case of some of the *C. persicifolia* cultivars, especially the doubles, is unnecessary.

Cuttings may also be taken, again preferably in the spring, when new growth is strong. Suitable media are a peat-and-sand, sand and vermiculite, or other proprietary cuttings mix, for preference in a propagator where watering is easily controlled. Some bottom heat may hasten root formation, it but is not essential. A clean cutting with lower leaves removed should be placed in the medium and watered in. Fresh green growth and firmness of hold in the propagator show that new roots have formed, when the new plants may be potted up. As campanulas are not at this stage hungry plants there is little need for transfer until good root formation is assured.

PESTS AND DISEASES

As a genus, campanula is outstandingly trouble-free in cultivation. The primary enemy is the slug, with his cousin the snail,

but they are as a general rule only troublesome with some of the more succulent (and, of course, rare and valuable) smaller species. In particular, a slug of 3mm in length can decimate a pan of seedlings in a night, or eat out the growing bud of a delicate plant as rapidly. Various authorities place faith in various slug-baits, whilst other refute them just as stoutly. Precautions such as the placing of plants, standing seed trays on the very sharpest of sands (silver sand, for example) seem as effective as any. Aluminium sulphate (now sold under various patent names) in powder or solution around the plants at risk has proved useful; this has the advantage that it is not toxic to pets, birds or earthworms, but sprinkling on the foliage should be avoided. The species particularly at risk are indicated in the descriptive texts, but it must be emphasised that the vast majority are not greatly menaced.

Aphids rarely trouble campanulas, even when they are abundant on nearby plantings.

Rusts have been described in the literature, and although we have not often seen them in 20-odd years of growing campanulas, rust has mostly frequently been seen on *C. persicifolia*. If they should occur, a general book of plant pests should be consulted (*Collins Guide to the Pests, Diseases and Disorders of Garden Plants*, Buczacki and Harris, is readily available). Campanula rust, *Puccinia campanulae*, fulfills its entire life-cycle on *Campanula* species and on *Jasione montana*. Another rust, *Coleosporum tussilaginis*, also attacks some species of campanula, but this alternates in its life-cycle between *Campanula* and *Pinus sylvestris*, and so it is important not to grow the pine in the vicinity of campanulas, or, as some would say, vice-versa! Rust is most troublesome on *C. persicifolia*, and especially in the weaker double forms. It is easily missed in the early stages, as it starts on the undersides of the leaves, showing as small orange pustules. These pustules can also be found on the stems, and even flowers. Later, blotches appear on the upper surfaces of the leaves, and the plant can be defoliated. All dead foliage should be removed. A vigorously growing plant will resist the disease, and good culture is important. An excess of nitrogenous fertiliser should, however, be avoided, as this results in soft leafy growth that is susceptible to rust attack. A proprietary fungicide containing bupirimate with triforine, mancozeb or penconazole can be applied at the first sign of attack, and then repeated as necessary. Preparations currently available in Britain containing these fungicides are Miracle Nimrod-T, Bio Dithane 945, and Murphy Tumbleblite II. One of us has eradicated rust by leaving plants in pots exposed over winter to hard frost, which has killed the rust and left the campanulas unharmed. Organic cultivation methods may be a help here.

In the same general way damping-off of seedlings may be encountered; though not commonly. Precautions such as sowing seed thinly and not over-watering will usually be quite adequate.

Reference
1. John Innes compost is seven parts sterilised loam, three parts moss peat or peat substitute such as coir, two parts sharp sand, with limestone and fertiliser added according to the plant's stage of development.

THE PLANTS

C. ABIETINA Grisebach.

60cm x 30cm • Violet • July

Rosettes of oval leaves, wider at the base, or broadly lance-shaped leaves, are 5cm long on short petioles, and give rise to a number of fine stems bearing longer, narrower and stemless leaves, often more abundant at the tops. The stems and leaves are hairless. The flower, about 2-3cm across and of a colour variously described as light violet or reddish-violet, is a wide open bell, the petals spreading from the centre like the spokes of a wheel. The calyx, about one-third the length of the corolla lobes, is awl-shaped, smooth, not toothed or cut, and without appendages.

C. abietina occurs in stony mountain grassland in the Carpathian and North Balkan mountains; also in the Caucasus.

Flora Europaea makes C. abietina a subspecies of C. patula, a somewhat coarser biennial plant of lower elevations throughout Europe. Whereas C. patula is biennial, C. abietina is markedly perennial, even if not a long-lived one. A clear sign of this is that it throws stolons, but from the point of view of the gardener not menacingly so, as with certain other species of campanula.

C. abietina is an attractive, if somewhat neglected, plant suited for the front of the border, where its relative delicacy is appreciated. It sets seed well, and may be easily propagated from winter or early spring sowing; or alternatively, divided annually, when it appreciates a rich but well-drained soil. The plant received an AM in 1891.

Synonyms: C. Patula L. Ssp. abietina (Grisebach) Simonkai; C. vajdae Penzes.

C. ADSURGENS

See C. arvatica.

C. 'ALASKANA'

50cm • Blue • June/Aug

This is a large variant of C. rotundifolia in all its parts. Botanically it is merged with that species, as is the somewhat similar C. r. var. groenlandica, referred to especially in American literature. These come, of course, from Alaska and Greenland respectively, although they are probably dispersed over wider areas than just these. C. rotundifolia var. alaskana as usually offered may be a large-flowered form of uncertain origin.

C. ALLIARIIFOLIA Willd.

60cm x 45cm • White • July/Oct

A tuft of heart-shaped leaves, on stalks up to 20cm long, forms the base of Campanula alliariifolia. This throws up a clump of leafy stems, occasionally branching and bearing a one-sided raceme of flowers up to 5cm in length, narrowly bell-shaped and white or creamy-white in colour, though the wild type is given as purplish-white, a shade rare in cultivation. The corolla segments are about one-fifth of the petal's entire length, with softly hairy circular appendages. The three-part style is not exserted beyond the corolla.

Campanula alliariifolia

This is not the most elegant of campanulas, but it is hardy, soundly perennial and long-lasting. The basal clump of leaves is fairly coarse, but not undecorative in itself; these leaves are felted above and quite woolly beneath, the leaf-margin slightly toothed and looking characteristically somewhat crumpled when young. It is not at all fussy as to soil, but does not need a rich one. It tends in our experience to stand up better in a poor soil when grown in exposed and windy positions. It also gives a better effect when a clump of three or five are placed together. It seeds itself abundantly.

C. alliariifolia occurs in Anatolia, Turkey, and in the Caucasus, growing in open scrub and conifer forests, occasionally on cliffs, but frequently on steep banks; in fact it appears to its best advantage if it can be placed at the top of a bank. The flowering period is long, and it will repeat well if dead-headed.

Propagation is easiest by seed – it sows itself modestly; seed is set abundantly. Division in spring is also easy.

C. a. 'Ivory Bells'

This was originally a selection distributed by Alan Bloom, and given as being of more compact habit, and with larger basal leaves, than the type. Unfortunately, seedlings are variable, and this has by default become a vernacular name for the species rather than a cultivar designation.

Synonyms: *C. lamiifolia* Adam.; *C. macrophylla* Sims.

C. ALPESTRIS All.

12cm • Blue • June

This comes from lime-free screes in the Western Alps. Fine underground runners slowly form a straggling mat by throwing up tiny rosettes of longish, narrow leaves, often slightly folded in on the central veins and with wavy margins. The almost invisible resting bud of winter opens up in the spring, and the rosette throws up a central stem which bears one, but occasionally several, flowers of a good bell shape and mid-blue, large for the size of the plant and length of stem. The flowers are often held in a characteristic horizontal fashion, are somewhat narrowed at the base, and the five calyx lobes are narrow with sharp points and half the corolla length.

This is a sought-after plant, long-lived and not difficult in cultivation, if given very good drainage but plentiful watering during the flowering period. Although it occurs naturally on lime-free mountains, it does not appear to be too fussy in the garden. It may be grown satisfactorily in a pot, but, like many others, in order to keep it in character should be potted on regularly. It is an ideal sink plant.

C. a. 'Alba'

Known, though rare, and less robust.

C. a. 'Grandiflora'

In circulation, but if this is correctly named the flower appears slightly clumsy for the size of the plant. It is, however, a strong grower which is easily propagated from its abundant runners.

C. a. 'Rosea'

An undistinguished pink, tending to muddy, and usually of uncertain constitution.

The type was awarded an AM in 1987; *C. a.* 'Alba' received the same award back in 1930, while a form shown as *C.a.* 'Frank Barker' received an AM, also in 1930, but this appears to be lost today.

Synonym: *C. allionii* Vill.

C. ANCHUSIFLORA Sibth. & Smith
30cm x 25cm • Blue • summer

This is one of the grey, or silver-hairy campanulas from Eastern Greece, occurring on limestone rock. A substantial taproot forms a flat rosette of lyrate leaves. In this respect it is similar to *C. rupestris*, *C. topaliana* and others, and Crook groups them together. The rosette, which is decorative enough to be grown for its own sake, gradually enlarges, and after one to three seasons' growth (generally two) hairy stems arise and branch shortly to bear many blue tubular bells of a pale shade. There is often a taller central main stem and diffuse semi-erect side stems. The flower is also hairy; the calyx lobes are triangular with very small appendages. The style bears five stigmas.

Campanula anchusiflora is very much more hardy than its origins would suggest, and we have seen it safely through winters of repeated frosts down to some -12°C (10°F). It prefers some shelter, however –

preferably that of an alpine house – to give of its very best. It is satisfactory in a pot, provided that this is not too shallow - the taproot needs adequate accommodation.

Although the plant, like many others of similar origin, is monocarpic, dying after flowering, seed is set abundantly, and the species may be kept going in cultivation by this means.

The following are mentioned by Crook as composing this group and few who have cultivated them will quarrel with him, especially when, as is so often the case, they are offered wrongly named. The distinctions within the *C. rupestris* aggregate appear to be largely geographical. For this reason it is worthwhile keeping a note of the place of origin if growing a plant from wild collected seed. The information will help to verify the correct name of the plant.

C. andrewsii A.DC

C. lyrata Lam.

C. betonicifolia Sibth. & Smith

C. rupestris Sibth, & Smith

C. celsii A. DC.

C. stricta L.

C. ephesia (DC.) Boiss.

C. tomentosa Lam.

C. hagielia Boiss.

C. topaliana Lam.

We have confined ourselves to the names endorsed by either *Flora Europaea* or P. Davis in *Flora of Turkey*, Vol. 6.

Campanula topaliana on Passava Fort, Mani, southern Greece

C. ARGYROTRICHA Wall

10cm x 15cm • smoky blue • Summer

This is one of the many Himalayan species which all tend to resemble each other. *C. argyrotricha* is a miniature with a tuft of roundish grey-green felted leaves and fine stems bearing one or two grey-blue hanging bells, often wider than their length. Grown in a pot in an alpine house it seeds profusely from year to year, both within and around the pot, to the point where one is not sure whether it is truly perennial or merely replacing itself with overwintering seedlings. It is ruggedly hardy, and though somewhat flimsy and small, an attractive miniature. It is best acquired as seed. It could be dubbed a minor version of *C. cashmiriana*.

C. ARVATICA Lag   AGM.
12cm × mat. • Blue, Violet • June/July

This is a sound perennial from the north of
Spain which slowly forms a close mat of
tufts of small, toothed rotund leaves on
short petioles. Stems of ten to 15cm height
bear a few similar leaves, and are topped,
usually singly, with pale blue, or violet stars
up to 25mm across for a long period in
June and July. In nature the plant is
invariably found growing among rocks; in
the garden it will be happy in a rock-
crevice or a scree of well-drained limestone
chippings, or even in tufa, though this will,
of course, restrict its spread and probably
limit its life. In the scree, which is probably
the simplest way of growing it, it will move
slowly and last many years in the open. *C.
arvatica* will do quite well in a pot, but will
need repotting, and breaking up at the
same time for propagation, every other
year or so. This is not a menacing runner.
An AM was obtained in 1952.

C. a. 'Alba'
This form is occasionally offered. It is
attractive, with a clear white flower, and a
long-lived plant when grown in a limestone
scree. AM awarded in 1937.

C. a. var. *adsurgens*
This variant is a grey felted form of the
species and the flowers are grey-blue. It is
not as robust as the type, and much less
inclined to spread by underground runners.
It is found oin stony ground and walls in a
restricted area of the mountains of Leon in
Spain. Unfortunately, in cultivation it

crosses freely with the type, giving
intermediate forms which are less
attractive, and in practice the only means
of acquiring it is by wild collection of the
plant or seed.

Synonym: *C. adsurgens* Ler. & Lev.

C. AUCHERI A.DC.
15cm • Blue • June/July

There are a number of campanulas from
the Caucasus and Armenia which are so
similar that even in nature they are difficult
to distinguish. In cultivation they have
doubtless hybridised to the point where the
gardener, albeit an alpine devotee, will
accept Crook's verdict that they are quite
indistinguishable, and Ingwersen's
description: 'the confusing group... all
grading into each other to a bewildering
extent'. Peter Davis, in the *Flora of Turkey*
is of similar opinion; we are content to be
of the company.

When offered *C. aucheri*, *C. bellidifolia*,
C. saxifraga or *C. tridentata* we suggest
quiet acceptance of the label, provided that
the plant has dense rosettes of basal,
spoon-shaped leaves, more or less rotund,
with or without slight teeth at their tips
('tridentate'), the rosettes gradually
building up to a rounded cushion
particularly reminiscent of a dead
hedgehog, whilst dormant in winter. On
close examination, these rosettes reveal the
tiniest green buds which, amongst the first
of the campanulas, revive to flourish and to
throw up stems bearing open cups thrust to

the sun, usually a deep blue with a pale or even a white 'eye'. A happy plant will conceal all foliage beneath the flowers, held singly at the top of each sparsely leaved stem. The three-part style is shorter than the corolla, the calyx lobes are triangular-pointed, and the much smaller appendages also triangular. These are all lime-lovers or indifferent; alpine plants which may be grown equally well in pots, sinks or troughs, provided drainage is good, or in a hole in a tufa rock. Like most of their race, they appreciate a good collar of gravel or grit to protect them from winter damp, under which conditions they will prove to be trouble-free and long-lived. Scree conditions suit them well.

C. *aucheri*, as such, was awarded an AM in 1960; C. *tridentata* obtained an AM in 1935.

C. a. 'Quarry Wood'

Obtained an AM in 1965. We hope that this form is still in cultivation, but have not been able to trace it.

C. 'AVALON'

20cm x 30cm • Violet • July

This looks like a C. *carpatica*, and is not infrequently quoted as such. It was, however, and is when found, a cross between C. *Carpatica turbinata* and C. *raineri*. It is clearly intermediate between these two parents, of which the latter is the pollen parent (as opposed to C. 'Pseudoraineri', where the seed parent is C. *raineri*). These two are closely related, and

readily hybridise either way – all too readily, in many situations!

C. 'Avalon' has the habit of a neat C. *turbinata*, forming a close, tidy hummock of hairy stems and leaves; the flower is the open and full cup-shape of C. *raineri*. The leaves are mid-green, heart-shaped and pointed, with somewhat crinkled edges; the underside of the leaves and the long petioles are especially characterised by the fine stiff hairs. The flowers are borne as if resting on the cushion of foliage, which gives a particularly neat and beautiful effect. This plant is slow to spread and not particularly rich in offsets, which is surprising with the parents from which it arises, but this could be the main reason why it is not common. We doubt if the original is still in cultivation.

C. BARBATA L.

30cm x 10cm • Blue, White • Summer

This is a distinctive small campanula of the grass upper meadows of the Alps, also occurring in southwest Poland and one small area in Norway. It only occurs in nature in lime-free soils, and is no doubt happier – which means longer-lived, in practice – in the same in cultivation. In any case it tends to be short-lived, and for many is biennial. Being also a meadow plant, it shows evidence of being happier grown in company, looking well in a raised bed with tufts of miniature grass like *Festuca ovina* 'Glauca' or *F. glacialis*. A perennial taproot or stolon produces a tuft of lance-shaped leaves in spring, and this throws up one, or several, stems when established, bearing but a few strap-shaped leaves and usually several pendent flowers of lavender-blue. Deeper blue is rare, but white is not infrequent, much more so in cultivation than in nature. These flowers have lobes divided to one-third, reflexed to reveal the hairs within which form the beard of the specific name. The style bears three stigmas, the calyx lobes are triangular, with short, rounded, reflexed appendages.

The taproot demands a deep soil, but this should preferably not be rich. A deep pot, as opposed to an alpine half-pot, can produce a good plant which will last for several years, though it frequently proves biennial. Seed is usually abundantly set, and may be collected and used for propagation.

An AM was obtained in 1951.

Campanula barbata

C. BETULIFOLIA C. Koch   AGM

30cm x 40cm. • White/pink • June/Sept

Some fine forms of this plant have been collected as seed in recent years, and it is proving itself an adaptable and versatile subject which can be grown in the front of the border, on the rock-garden, in sinks or in pots with equal success. It justifies a prominent position where its charming delicate appearance can be appreciated. The name is a reference to the 'birch-like' appearance of the leaves.

A tuft of thick and glossy basal leaves arises from a perennial woody rhizome. These leaves are pale to mid-green, somewhat bluish, long heart- to wedge-shaped, with wavy indented margins. The petioles are somewhat longer than the leaf-blade. There arise from this tuft numerous wavy stems bearing more or less oval, toothed leaves, on long stalks. The stems are branched above, each branch bearing up to five flowers in a loose cluster. The buds are characteristically wine-red, and open up to a relatively large rounded bell, white or with a pinkish tinge, often heavy enough to make the branches somewhat floppy. In the best garden forms – it is a very variable plant – the corolla is of a good bell-shape and the stems sturdy enough to hold the flowering branches upright above the foliage. The calyx lobes are triangular with short appendages.

This is a soundly hardy perennial which was given an AM in 1937; in the plant then exhibited the flowers were of a pale pink. It now bears an AGM.

Cultivation presents no difficulty, so long as there is good drainage in the soil habitat; this should be moist but not too rich, as this tends to give excessive growth of leaf at the expense of flowers, which also become hidden in the foliage. It is a plant from varying elevations in Turkey, Armenia and the Caucasus, and the higher forms are reliably hardy provided that drainage is good and the roots do not freeze for too long in frosty weather.

C. finitima

This form falls within the above description, and there is little doubt that in common circulation there is no difference. In the original descriptions C. finitima was given as having more cup-shaped flowers than the narrower bells of C. betulifolia.

Similar species are C. troegerae and C. choruhensis, both quite recently described, and also occurring in Turkish and Russian Armenia. All three are grouped botanically in the Symphyandriformes section of Campanula – approaching Symphyandra in that the anthers are sometimes fused into a tube around the style, as in that genus; but here only in the young flower.

Synonyms: C finitima Fomin; Symphyandra finitima Fomin (C. betulaefolia)

C. 'BIRCH HYBRID' AGM

15-20cm • Blue • June/Sept

This plant, introduced by Walter Ingwersen, was initially shown as C. x *portenscharskyana*; it was awarded an AM, with a unsurprising recommendation that the name be changed. It is C. *portenschlagiana* x C. *poscharskyana*, fearsome names enough before hybridisation. The name 'Birch Hybrid' was resorted to after the nursery name, Birch Farm. In fact the use of the word hybrid is frowned upon under nomenclature rules and *Campanula* 'Birch Farm' would probably be a better name. This is a strong-growing small campanulas with a particularly long flowering period, and rightly very popular. It has been awarded an AGM.

Strongly toothed kidney-shaped basal leaves on long petioles throw up branching stems bearing an abundance of pale mauve bells with spreading lobes divided to one-third their length. The style with its three stigmas is shorter than the flower tube.

Crook refers to this plant as similar to a major form of C. *portenschlagiana* in cultivation. In general it is a tidier plant, and, although claiming affinity with C. *poscharskyana*, certainly does not have the long branching stems of that species, nor the invasive propensities of the former. It behaves well in a pot, but will need frequent moving on; breaking off the numerous rooted stems at the same time will give abundant progeny.

C. BONONIENSIS L.

76cm x 50cm • Blue • July

This is a greyish plant whose leaves have short soft hairs. It has a basal rosette of stalked, heart-shaped leaves, about 7cm long which throws up a stem bearing leaves which become progressively shorter toward the tip; these are stalkless and partly clasp the stem at the leaf-axils. There is a long spike-like branch of smallish flowers, clustered in twos or threes on short pedicels. The flowers are smooth, funnel-shaped, the lobes divided to about one-third their length, and are blue. The lance-shaped calyx-lobes are much shorter than the petals, and very bristly. The style is in three parts and about the same length as the corolla. The flowers, and the subsequent seed-capsules, are pendent.

C. *bononiensis* occurs over a widespread area and conditions: Central and Eastern Europe, Iran, Caucasus and Western Siberia, at forest margins, scrub and rocky ground. It was first described from the Bologna area of Italy, hence the name; Bononia being the Latin form.

Such a widespread plant cannot be delicate, and it is not hard to suit, accepting virtually any soil, in sun or shade. Crook condemns it to the more extensive wild garden and also assures us that it is biennial. *Flora Europaea* and *Flora of Turkey* give it as perennial. It would seem to us that some clones are more permanent than others, and also a rich soil tends to spoil it away quicker. Whilst it is not an aristocrat of the border, a good cluster can be effective. Graham Stuart

Thomas refers to it as a refined plant with graceful spires; a good form is just that.

While it may be divided in spring as growth restarts, propagation will not prove prolific by this method, but seed is set freely and germinates well. The species is not long-lived in the garden.

Synonym: *C. ruthenica* Bieb.

C. 'BURGHALTII' AGM
60cm x 30cm • Purple/grey • July/Sept

This, a very old hybrid whose origins and history are lost, is generally accepted to be a cross between *C. punctata* and *C. latifolia*. It has more of the form of the seed parent, that is, *C. punctata*, than of the pollen parent, *C. latifolia*. It is, in fact, the reverse cross to C. 'Van Houttei'.

The basal leaves are heart-shaped, on stalks as long as the leaf-blades, and very slightly winged. Up the stem the leaves become progressively more oval, wider at

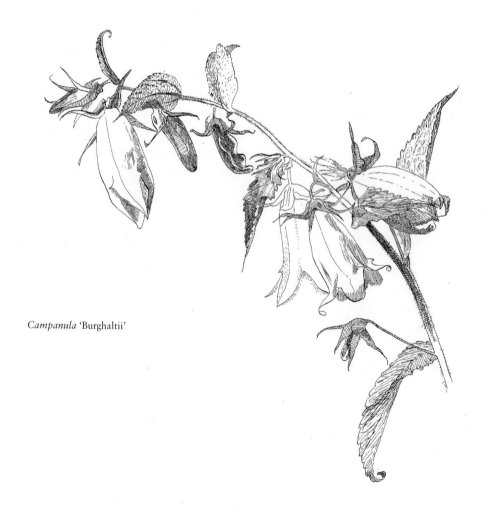

Campanula 'Burghaltii'

the base, lance-shaped and also stalkless. The upper surface of the leaves is smooth, but there are short bristly hairs on the veins of the underside, and also on the stems. These are somewhat branched, and the flowers are borne terminally in each leaf axil. The stem-leaves are usually very pointed and upward-facing like ears. The flowers are amethyst-purple in bud. About two-thirds of the way from the tip of the bud is a little hook in each lobe. When the flowers open this marks the point at which each lobe is split. They are slightly hairy within and dove grey to pearly lilac when fully expanded. However, they do not open widely, and form a long narrow bell some 7-10cm long. The spent flowers change colour again to a true blue as they die. The calyx lobes are long-pointed with reflexed triangular appendages. The three-part style does not protrude.

Evidence of hybrid origin is the fact that seed is not set, so the only means of increase is division in spring, or by taking fresh spring growths from the rootstock which establish easily. This is a sought-after plant and always in short supply, as it does not spread anything like as vigorously as the *punctata* parent. It is said of it that it has a slightly running rootstock, but there is little evidence of this in a heavy soil; in moist open soil this quality might show itself. In any case, C. 'Burghaltii' prefers some moisture, and is best in part shade, where, when happy, it will flower for months continuously. John Raven, in a *A Botanist's Garden*, touches on it; 'instead of lifting its many spires straight upwards... it

sprays them gracefully in all directions so that it is appreciably wider than tall - and its large pendent flowers are of a unique and soft shade that is quite as much pale grey as blue.' [1]

C. 'Burghaltii' is a long-lasting perennial and soundly hardy. Like many another campanula it is completely deciduous, and its position should be well marked in the border before ambitious winter or early spring tidying-up is undertaken.

C. CALAMINTHIFOLIA Lam.
3cm x 40cm • Lilac • Summer

This plant is all too often confused with C. *sartorii*, the latter taking its place in the trade. It is at best a short-lived perennial, whilst C. *sartorii*, which as a plant or grown from seed it often turns out to be, is quite relentlessly biennial (and sets seed and sows itself much more prolifically). A tiny rosette of slightly toothed heart-shaped leaves puts out ground-hugging, decumbent stems up to 20cm or so long, profusely furnished with small, rounded sessile leaves, and with upright slightly funnel-shaped lilac bells. The whole plant is greyish with fine hairs – a sure mark of its origin in the Greek Aegean islands. The style is longer than the corolla and ends in three stigmas. The calyx is made up of five triangular lobes, with small triangular appendages.

This species, in a very well-drained position, will survive an average hard English winter outside, but is seen at its best in an alpine house. It is a lime-lover, and looks particularly well clambering over tufa rock; it is equally content in a limestone scree, but is not long lived.

C. *calaminthifolia* is related, and similar in habit, to C. *heterophylla*, but this latter has distinctly spoon-shaped leaves, and is less hairy and grey.

Synonym: C. *sartorii* Boiss, & Heldr.

C. CARPATHA Halacsy
20 cm x 25 cm • Blue • Summer

This plant, little known or grown until recently, comes from the island of Karpathos, to the northeast of Crete, where it grows in shady, rocky places. Like most of the Greek species, from both mainland and island, it is a lime-lover.

A tuft of long spoon-shaped darkish green and slightly felted leaves, strongly veined, round-toothed on the margins, and on short-winged petioles, throws up several stems which may be upright or more or less prostrate. These bear similar sessile stem-leaves and, in their axils as well as at the tips, tubular bells of a rich blue or blue-violet. These are cleft to about one-third, and the lobes of the 2cm long flower only recurve slightly. There are five stigmas; the calyx lobes are triangular; the prominent appendages roundish.

C. *carpatha* is biennial or monocarpic, and though it consequently dies after flowering, it usually sets seed well, and may be easily propagated by this means.

Two species from Crete are similar:

C. *tubulosa* Lam.

Occurs in the western mountains of Crete on limestone rocks and also in dampish places. It is hairier than C. *carpatha*, giving the leaves a darker and greyer appearance. The stems tend to branch more, the flowers are a little longer and they are of a paler lilac shade.

C. *pelviformis* Lam.

Occurs in the more easterly area of Crete; it appears as a smaller form of C. *tubulosa*.

Both C. *carpatha* and C. *tubulosa* have an AM to their credit, received in 1952 and 1933 respectively.

C. CARPATICA Jacq.   AGM
To 45cm x 45cm • Blue/White • Summer

Campanula carpatica has suffered some neglect in the past by falling into that ill-defined no-man's-land between the rock garden and the border where the dedicated devotee of each has left its promotion to the other. The least disturbed by such treatment or lack of it, however, is the plant itself: in its carefree resilience it will be equally happy wherever it is grown.

Coming from the Carpathian Mountains, as the name suggests (and to be carefully distinguished from the last-mentioned species), C. *carpatica* has a perennial rootstock which throws up a tuft, and, when well established, a clump, of bright green roundish leaves which, as with a number of other species, disappear as the stems grow, to be replaced by more oval to triangular ones on long petioles. These are

Campanula carpatica 'Hannah'

repeated up the stems, becoming more heart-shaped, the petioles gradually diminishing. Toothing of the leaf-margin varies, as does the amount of branching of the flower-stems. The flowers are borne terminally. Because this species is very variable in the wild it has, along with *C. persicifolia*, attracted attention from the florists in the past, and a large number of clones have been selected and named: thus form and size of plant, and shape and colour of flower are consequently very variable. In the wild type-plant the flower is a pale narrow bell, but in cultivation colour is between purple and white, and the shape anything from funnel to cup to umbrella to open salver. The short wide corolla lobes are sometimes rounded, and others bear star-shaped points; the flower is held boldly to the sun. The calyx-teeth are lance-shaped, and there are no appendages. The style divides into three.

C. carpatica is a sun-lover, and ideal for the front of a well-drained border. Its cultivation is in general of the easiest, and it will thrive where it is free from winter waterlogging. It is very free-flowering, and if 'shorn' as the flowers fade will give a second crop, equally good, later. In fact it is one of the longest-flowering campanulas. This is not an invasive species, though some plants appear to seed more easily (or successfully) than others; it will, with a minimum of attention, give a minimum of trouble with a maximum of effect in the garden. Its detractors should note that it has received an AGM, more than they can claim for themselves !

C. turbinata

A form variously described as *C. turbinata* or *C. carpatica* subsp. *turbinata* is said to be dwarfer and with unbranched stems, the flowers being the shape of spinning tops ('turbinata'). The influence of the form is seen in some of the named cultivars.

More than a dozen cultivars have over the years received Awards of Merit, incidentally breaking the record of any other campanula. A by no means exhaustive search of literature and lists will quickly turn up as many as 50 cultivar names of varying authority and worth, but many of those of impeccable derivation and pedigree have been lost, some of the AM winners among them. It should, of course, be noted that no named cultivar may be had true from seed; when offered, such are at best only strains, however little variation they may show. Propagation may be by seed, or by cuttings in spring as growth restarts. Only by vegetative propagation may the cultivars be had true to name; which, of course, applies to any species of any genus.

When the total number of species of campanula in cultivation is taken into account, there are relatively few hybrids about – the operative word being 'relatively'. In the wild they are virtually unknown, but are commoner under garden conditions. Of those species which do tend to hybridise, *C. carpatica* is certainly one of the more promiscuous, most of the progeny being on the rock garden scale. It must be said that in the list of cultivars given here there will be a few whose exact origins are now untraceable, though an intelligent guess may be hazarded. The following are among the more readily available cultivars in the UK. The dwarf forms, mostly derived from the subspecies *turbinata*, with a single flower to a stem, are both ideal and easy for a sink or trough. Careful treatment will produce good pot-plants also, and such use is popular on the Continent – but they will need regular feeding to be a success. Suitable cultivars include *C. c.* 'Hannah' and *C. c.* 'Karl Foester'.

C. c. 'Blue Clips' (Benary)

China blue cups on a 15-20cm hummock; this is a very reliable plant which in fact comes very nearly true from seed.

C. c. 'Blue Moonlight' (Bloom)

Appropriately named very pale blue open

saucers in a dense hummock; very free-
flowering, 20-25cm.

C. c. 'Bressingham White' (Bloom)

Selected by Alan Bloom, this has open
white flowers with a blue-green trace at the
base of the petals. 20cm. Received an AM
in 1967.

C. c. 'Chewton Joy' (Prichard)

Received an AM in 1929, and is still going
strong. It is about 20cm, free- and late-
flowering; open cups of china blue with
paler centre.

C. c. 'Craven Bells' (Farrer)

Probably from Farrer's nursery, and an old
selection, with china blue flowers of very
round shape.

C. c. 'Hannah'

Though the flowers are relatively small they
are borne so abundantly and at a time
when greatly appreciated - late summer,
and are of such a good white that this
cultivar, which is almost certainly of
turbinata parentage, is outstanding. It
forms a cushion of 20 x 30cm when
established.

Campanula carpatica 'Chewton Joy'

Campanula carpatica 'Isabel'

C. c. 'Isabel' (Prichard)

This one of the many successful Prichard campanula introductions, a seedling from *C. c.* 'Riverslea' in 1905, and therefore again of *turbinata* origins. It is a deep blue, flat flower, described originally as purple-blue, about 25cm in height, and its longevity in cultivation is evidence of a sound constitution. AM 1904.

C .c. 'Jewel'

Of German origin, probably Benary. Deep purple flower on a compact plant; a slow spreader.

C. c. 'Karl Foerster'

At 20cm with large, open, deep cobalt blue saucers, this is named after the respected German plantsman, himself responsible for many good plant introductions. It flowers early and has been forced for the Chelsea Flower Show, when it looks what it thus becomes, a house-plant. It is, however, robust and long-flowering and, like many listed here, fitted for the front of the border as much as for a pot.

C. c. 'Maureen Haddon' (Bloom)

Named after one of the staff at Bressingham. Masses of smallish flowers of an even mid-blue.

C. c. 'Mrs V Frere'

Flowers are of flat, rotate shape with finely chiselled dimpled petals, similar to 'Isabel' but smaller, paler blue; it would make a fine model for a five-part hors d'oeuvre dish. It was lost, but has been recently rediscovered in Sussex.

Campanula carpatica 'Jewel'

C. c. 'Riverslea'

Prichards introduced this, and it is almost certainly the 'Giant', alias 'Riverslea Giant', which obtained an AM when shown in 1931. It was described as a little over 30cm with large flat deep purple-blue flowers 5cm in diameter. It is not now easy to find – a fate shared with many a worthy cultivar – but it is still available.

C. c. 'Snowdrift'

This is a good clean white flower of a medium size; a slow-growing plant, compact in form.

C. c. 'Suzie'

This recent selection bears large pale blue flowers on a low-growing plant.

C. c. 'White Clips' (Benary)

Like its blue counterpart, an introduction

from the German Benary nursery, and a strain which comes fairly true from seed; it bears a clear white flower held some 25cm high on a tidy plant.

C. c. 'White Star' (Prichard)

Received an AM in 1905, again from the Prichard nursery at Riverslea. It is of open form in flower, with characteristic pointed tips to the star-shaped corolla lobes, satiny white in texture, held about 30cm high. This is no longer easy to find.

Many other cultivars are now also hard if not impossible to find, but among them the following would be worth tracking down:

'Big Ben'
'Harvest Moon'
'Blue Bonnet' (AM 1968)
'Lilliput'
'Blue Star'
'Little Gem'
'China Cup'
'Loddon Bell'
'Clarence Elliott'
'Loddon Fairy' (AM 1967)
'Claribel'
'Queen of Somerville'
'Convexity' (HC)
'The Pearl' (AM 1967)
'Far Forest'

Campanula carpatica 'White Star'

'White Convexity' (AM 1947)

'Glacier Blue'

'White Gem'

'Grandiflora' (AM 1967)

Without wishing to appear cynical, we have to say that our experience has taught us that many plants offered under any of these names could need careful checking for authenticity.

C. CASHMERIANA Royle
15cm • Blue • July/Sept

C. cashmeriana is an exception to the general rule, which is that Himalayan campanulas are of little garden worth. To the enthusiastic grower of mountain plants who is familiar with the great range of wonderful plants from there, this may come as something of a surprise. We have observed, however, that environments which favour primulas are not those chosen by campanulas. Campanula and dianthus, however, are soul mates. These generalisations also transfer to the garden; here, however, we can manipulate micro-climates within relatively small areas, to the advantage of many sorts of plants which would otherwise choose very different conditions.

C. cashmeriana is a small wiry deciduous campanula which springs each year from a woody rootstock thrust by choice deep into narrow rock crevices. Fine stems covered with a white pubescence are held erect or trailing and sparsely furnished with elliptical, grey-hairy leaves. The stems are lightly branched above, and each terminates with a solitary pendent bell of aristocratic shape; they are of a grey-blue shade, again because of their fine hairiness. In a good clone they will be some 15cm long and wide, which, as they are profusely borne on a relatively small plant, make for a fair show. To this must be added that the flowering period is as long as that of any campanula in cultivation; each year we have them, in a sheltered spot, from July up to and into the frosts. Seed is set with moderate enthusiasm, and they will self-sow, especially in a sand-plunge, from which they may be transplanted. Seed is exceedingly fine, and not at all easy to gather by hand.

We have a soft spot for this little campanula, which is not nearly so often seen as it deserves, for it is not hard to grow. However, we have to add that there are unattractive forms about; it is said that it hybridises with some of the poorer Himalayan campanulas (there are a multitude of names covering annuals and short-lived perennials, all of which resemble *C. cashmeriana* to a greater or lesser extent).

C. cashmeriana was awarded an AM in 1958.

C. CESPITOSA Scop.
12cm • Blue • July

This species is similar to *C. cochlearifolia*, and all too often one receives the latter in its stead, especially from seed. There are clear differences. *C. cespitosa* is a tufted

Campanula cespitosa　　　　　　　　　*Opposite: Campanula* 'Constellation'

plant, arising from a single taproot, and with no tendency to spread by underground runners as does, so generously, *C. cochlearifolia*. *C. cespitosa* is generally taller in the stem, the flower is usually pinched in at the mouth, and the overall impression is of a less dainty plant. The blue is variable, but mid-blue is by far the most common. *C. cespitosa* is much less widespread in nature, being found only in limestone screes and among rocks in the Eastern Alps and in the mountains of the former Yugoslavia.

Propagation must be from spring cuttings, or from seed, and cultivation is quite straightforward, preferably in scree conditions.

C. CHAMISSONIS Fed.

to 20cm • Blue • June/Aug

This is a sound, easily grown and long-lasting species which occurs over a wide area which includes Japan, Siberia, Sakhalin, the Kuriles, Kamchatka, the Aleutians and Alaska. This is a wider area of the globe than we are wont to realise; consequently variations in the forms of this plant are also great.

C c. pilosa, dasyantha, chamissonis and other close relatives are described in the literature, and there is considerable overlapping and difference of opinion, but we note that both Kew and the *Flora of the USSR* give *C. chamissonis* priority; we accept therefore this name as covering what to the alpine gardener and enthusiast will be forms of the same species. As they all require the same cultural treatment, our task is easier.

The plant has a stout perennial root which produces a rosette of usually evergreen, smooth glossy spoon-shaped leaves with delicate and clearly marked veining. The margins are finely notched. These rosettes spread by underground runners, and the maturer ones among them throw up stems furnished with a few similar but more rounded and stemless leaves, and bearing at their tips long or rounded upright bells. These may often be very large for the size of the plant, and they vary in their shade of blue, frequently from the outside to the inside of the corolla. The variation in colour may give the impression that each petal is striped almost like a gentian, sometimes quite dramatically so; frankly, in a campanula we prefer less drama! This is a sturdy, easy and attractive plant. In nature it grows more commonly on lime-free soils, and in cultivation will flower better if we follow this taste, though it is not fussy. In a mat of *C. chamissonis* there will always be a number of rosettes which do not flower, though all may do so eventually. Grown in a peaty compost with good drainage provided by plentiful grit, this subject spreads slowly and happily, but never outrageously.

In Japan this is a 'florist's' flower whose different forms have been given a series of names, often in the manner of honorific titles. In Europe we find forms labelled as 'Major', 'Superba' etc., and these are frequently offered as such in garden centres. In themselves they mean little, and although such names were doubtless correctly conferred initially, they have tended to rub off indiscriminately on all-comers to assist sales. However, *C. chamissonis* 'Superba' AGM has larger flowers.

C. c. 'Oyobeni' is a selected form from Japan which bears richly striped flowers, and reveals fewer non-flowering rosettes than the type.

Synonyms: *C. dasyantha* Bieb.; *C. pilosa* Pall.; *C. altaica* A.DC.

C. COCHLEARIIFOLIA Lam. AGM
10cm • Blue, White • June/Aug

The 'Fairies' Thimbles' thrives happily in crevices, scree-beds, sinks troughs, paths, paving, drives, walls and pretty well anywhere else, creeping and seeding joyously. Some consider it a menace and others just despise it. It is both the easiest

Campanula cochleariifolia

and daintiest of all campanulas; the world would be immeasurably the poorer without it. The cause of the 'problem' is the creeping and branching rhizome which throws up tufts of small round or heart-shaped leaves and stems with narrower leaves, topped by the 'thimbles' which vary considerably both in form and colour. In nature the commonest shade is a mid-blue, but white, grey-blue, china-blue and lilac are known. Farrer found and named one 'Miranda', and generously predicted that it was going to be one of the greatest of rock garden plants! It has pale bells on longer stems than the average, and one of its virtues is the length of its flowering period, from summer right through to autumn. 'Miss Willmott', selected in the garden of that lady in Warley, Essex, is a miniature mob-cap with slightly paler fringes.

This is a perennial with a slowly creeping rhizome. The basal leaves are just as above, and the erect stems bear similar leaves which are gradually reduced up the stems to stemless bracts. The nodding flowers are carried in a one-sided cluster, up to five in number, but sometimes only singly.

C. c. var. *alba* – pure white
C. c. 'Bavaria Blue' – dark blue, compact; offered as seed by Jelitto of Germany
C. c. 'Bavaria White' – pure white, compact; as the blue form. May both come true from seed.
C. c. 'Blue Tit' (Bloom) – china-blue.
C. c. 'Cambridge Blue' (Bloom) – clear light blue, as to be expected.

C. c. 'Elizabeth Oliver' – see below.
C. c. 'Flore Pleno' – double blue; this may well occur spontaneously, and is usually a pale blue.
C. c. 'Hallii' – a hybrid – see below under this name.
C. c. 'Haylodgensis' – another hybrid; see under this name.
C. c. 'Miranda' – the genuine plant, very rare, is between white, grey and blue.
C. c. 'Miss Willmott' – a mid greyish-blue with the faintest of silver fringes to the mob-cap.
C. c. 'Oakington Blue ' (Bloom) – mid-blue, with large flowers.
C. c. 'R B Loder' – a double; see below.
C. c. 'Silver Chimes' – silver-blue.
C. c. 'Tubby' – a wider bell, as wide as deep, and very aptly named. Mid-blue.
C. c. 'Warleyensis' – see below under this name.
C. c. 'White Baby' – as var. *alba*.

These and a multitude of others are widely offered, and many flower generously over a wide period. Looking again at nature, we could learn that this is a plant of rock-crevices and poor, gritty ground; it is both happy and restrained when we copy this environment in the garden. One of the authors grows it in a raised bed of nothing but gravel and sand – in a mixture straight from the quarry; it, with other campanulas, phloxes, including the Mexican ones, penstemons, and a host of other alpine plants, grows well, flowers well and

Campanula cochleariifolia 'Tubby'

60

persists, while showing perfect restraint in the spreading.

Two double forms are not uncommonly found, and though in general double flowers are not greatly admired by the establishment of the alpine world, here an exception should be made.

C. c. 'Elizabeth Oliver'
This appeared in a garden near Nottingham in about 1972. It is a very attractive powder blue with a multiple corolla about 12cm across.

C. c. 'R.B. Loder'
Barely distinguishable from the above, but slightly taller and with flowers of an ice-blue shade. It received an AM in 1922 when shown by Prichards.

See also **C. 'Marion Fisher'**

Synonyms: *C. pusilla* Haenke; *C. bellardii* All.

Campanula cochlearifolia 'Elizabeth Oliver'

C. COLLINA Bieb.

20cm x 15cm • Blue • Summer

A campanula which made Reginald Farrer wax lyrical – no hard task for him. 'One of the most gorgeous campanulas we have, with tufts of downy foliage scallop-edged and heart-shaped on longish footstalks, and then the graceful foot-high stems, gracefully carrying magnificent big bells of imperial purple, satiny and brilliant...' [2]

A modestly running rootstock gives copious long-pointed ovate leaves on long petioles, downy in texture and very slightly toothed, and throws up a 20cm stem with well-spaced leaves like those of the rosette and a one-sided raceme of pendent flowers. Petals are dark blue to blue-violet, and in the form of a longish, but full, pendulous bell, the hairy-edged lobes of which are split to half and curl well back. The calyx-lobes are lance-shaped, not reflexed, and without appendages. The three-part style does not protrude beyond the petals.

Campanula collina does not appear to be fussy, and will grow equally well in limy or lime-free soil, though it is reported as coming from mainly granitic soils. It grows wild only in Armenia. In cultivation it does like a moister soil than is suggested by the pastures and rocky soils of its origin (it does not grow in rocks), and it will quickly succumb if the soil dries out in the garden. Drainage should be good. In a good, open loam it will spread, though never menacingly. It takes neither the eye nor the pen of a Farrer to appreciate the gorgeousness of a mat of it in flower, though its flowering is not long. It is one of the campanulas which, being completely deciduous and leaving no trace of its winter hiding-place, does not revel in being dug about while resting, but does appreciate a good mulch both in recognition and in encouragement. Propagation is easy by division in spring, or from seed.

The plant figures in the *Botanical Magazine* at t. 927 in 1806. It is a very variable species; several naturally occurring varieties have been described, and that depicted in the above was given as the 'Major' form, which does not now appear to be available.

C. 'CONSTELLATION'

15cm x 60cm • Violet-blue • June/Aug

This is probably a hybrid between *C. garganica* and *C. poscharskyana*. Found as a seedling and introduced by Alan Bloom, it has larger leaves than these putative parents and they tend to be more pointed, and more heavily toothed. It is an uninvasive clump-former, throwing out a mass of 45cm arms each season which bear many deep blue, star-shaped flowers larger than those of either parents. The calyx lobes are not reflexed, and the style appears not to divide at its tip; seedlings are not found and we have not been able to collect seed. For propagation, of course, this is not important, especially as division in spring is very easy, as are cuttings if necessary.

It is similar to C. 'E K Toogood', mentioned later, but lacks the white eye of the latter. Both make excellent hanging-basket subjects.

Campanula collina

Opposite: Campanula 'Constellation'

C. DIVARICATA Michx.

90cm • Pale blue • July/Aug

It appears strange that, relatively speaking, so few North American plants are common in cultivation, when in the wild there is such abundance, and when those from countries which have been less systematically botanised are so well known. Perhaps in the Americas there is not the widely dispersed love of gardening known in Britain and parts of Europe; and on the gardening, as opposed to the botanical, level, reliance there has been placed on European tastes and literature, with a consequent neglect of American natives. But is the grass always greener over the fence? Whatever the answer, we are now learning, none too soon, that the great American continent has a lot to offer the lover of flowers, and the situation is changing dramatically, especially in North American climates similar to Europe, such as the North-West.

Clifford Crook in his monograph described this species as being of considerable charm. Whilst North America is not strong in campanulas, this one could justifiably be depicted as its best. It is a perennial from the Southern Appalachian Mountains from Maryland south to Georgia, occurring on stony banks in both sun and shade.

Campanula divaricata forms clusters of rosettes of dark green oblong or lance-shaped leaves which taper at both ends to a sharp point. Smooth slender upright stems with few or no leaves branch repeatedly and bear toward their tips panicles of numerous small flowers (1cm long or less). These are pendent pale blue bells, each shaped not unlike those of some forms of *C. cochlearifolia*, and reminiscent of an old-fashioned mob-cap. The three part style extends beyond the petals by as much as the petal length, giving a strangely characteristic profile, for the long-styled campanulas usually have a circular or star-shaped corolla. In bell-ringing terms, the clapper protrudes way out beyond the bell! The calyx, like the rest of the plant, is smooth, with narrow pointed lobes that have no appendages.

This species presents no difficulty in cultivation, and generally sets abundant seed. It is not readily available as a plant, and seed from one of the alpine societies' seedlists is probably the only source.

C. *flexuosa* Michx.

This form has been described, and appears to be but a more compact alpine form of the type; to some this would be even more desirable. Some consider this to be only a synonym.

C. 'E.K. TOOGOOD'

20cm x 60cm • Violet • Summer

This is a presumed hybrid, but of uncertain origin. It is like a large and lush version of *C. garganica*, and could well owe something to *C. poscharskyana*. It throws out robust leafy branches from a rosette of strongly toothed, heart-shaped leaves, quite smooth and green, which bear bright blue, star-shaped flowers along their length. The lobes of the corolla are deeply divided, and the base of the flower, the 'eye', is a contrasting white. The style, which shares the white base and blue extremity, protrudes well out, and ends in three stigmas. The long-pointed calyx lobes reflex on to the ovary and the short stalk.

This campanula, which is quite freely available, makes a fine display especially growing on a wall; it flowers over a long period, and as already mentioned, displays well in hanging baskets. Shorn after flowering, it will readily repeat.

C. ELATINES L.

15cm x 30cm • Blue • Summer

This belongs to a group which includes the well-known *C. garganica*, and also *C. elatinoides*.

All have small round to heart-shaped leaves, usually not more than 1cm wide. These are delicately toothed, the basal ones on longish petioles, the stem-leaves having ever shorter stalks up the stem, which are semi-prostrate or rising. The flowers are finely-shaped stars on short pedicels along the full length of the stem. In general these are all neat, compact plants which do well either on the open rockery or in pots, being lime-lovers and weather-resistant. They are almost completely deciduous.

In an endeavour to simplify the group, and at the risk of overdoing simplicity, we describe the following from among the plants which are commonly offered. The *Plant Finder* has been our guide in this as in many matters.

C. elatines

More compact; the leaves are thicker and rounder, the flowers are not so showy. The whole plant is finely hairy, but not enough to be grey. A good form has a strong white base to the petals.

C. elatinoides

Very densely hairy and grey, with again the thicker leaves and with more numerous but smaller flowers; it is now classified as a subspecies of *C. elatines*.

C. fenestrellata

Very evidently of this same group. The leaves are a bright green, larger than any of the foregoing, and heavily toothed. The stems of this plant tend to be slightly ascending, as opposed to the ground-hugging, procumbent stems of *C. garganica*. *Flora Europaea* helps here by saying that the pollen of *C. fenestrellata* is blue, whilst that of *C. garganica* is yellow. The observant grower will generally also note that *C. fenestrellata* has longer stems, with smaller flowers than *C. garganica*.

Most possible permutations of the

Left: *Campanula fenestrellata*

names of members of this group have been made at various times by different authorities, and the following names as found in *Flora Europaea* are among the more commonly met, albeit with varying status:

C. elatines L.

C. elatinoides Moretti

C. garganica Ten. **subsp. acarnanica**
  subsp. cephallenica
  subsp. garganica

C. fenestrellata Feer **subsp. debarensis**
  subsp. fenestrellata
  subsp. istriaca

C. EXCISA Schleicher

15cm • Blue • July-Aug

This species, although probably not amongst the easiest, nor very long-lived in cultivation, is nonetheless attractive and popular because, like *C. zoysii*, it is just that little bit different! It is only found in a quite restricted area of the South Central Alps of Switzerland, in the Monte Rosa, Matterhorn, Simplon Pass triangle. It is a rambler in the style of *C. rotundifolia*, and among the rocks and screes in which it occurs it throws up thin wiry stems laxly clothed with narrow, smooth-edged leaves terminating in single, usually pendent, tubular bells with flared and pointed lobes, between which are the curious round punched-out holes which have given the plant its name. The stems are only about 8-10cm in height in nature, but in cultivation tend to be somewhat taller.

This is a real rambler, and so not happy kept in a pot for long. The ideal spot would be a granite scree containing a little peat below, for, as Farrer remarked, although the best plants are found in sunny spots, there is always some moisture beneath. Semi-shade, or a position where the mid-day sun in summer is shaded, is a fair compromise, but it must also have room to travel; otherwise it will be very short-lived in cultivation. In our experience *C. excisa* should not be allowed to dry out completely in winter, but equally should not be allowed to get too wet.

Propagation is from seed and rooted runner-cuttings in spring. This species is always found on lime-free scree, and lime should be avoided in its culture.

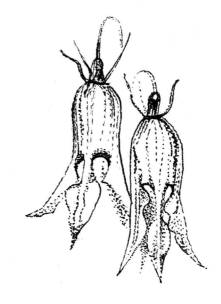

Campanula excisa flowers

C. FORMANEKIANA Degen & Doerfler   AGM

30cm • White • July/Aug

There are a number of campanulas from Greece, the Balkans, and what are considered the warmer areas of Southern Europe, which, because of their woolly 'finish', give the impression of being tender or fragile. In practice it is not as simple as this, for in the great majority of cases they are not afraid of the cold in itself, or even of prolonged freezing temperatures, but will suffer from alternate freezing and thawing if it is their roots that are concerned. If C. *formanekiana* is placed well up in a wall or well-drained rockery so that its roots are kept dry and unfrozen, and it will give a wonderful display.

A stout taproot forms a silver-grey rosette of particularly neatly arrayed leaves, reminiscent of the neatness of a Sempervivum. These are oval with a wider heart-shaped base, and slightly rounded at the apex. The petioles are long and winged. Normally, an upright central stem is accompanied by a number of lower, decumbent branches. The stem leaves have shorter and shorter petioles up the stem, and are also smaller. The flowers are large 'Canterbury Bells', about 4cm long, in white, pale pink or, very occasionally, pale blue, with a three part style. They are held erect and have large triangular calyx segments without any appendages.

This is a Balkan species which grows in the mountains of Macedonia. It was first collected by Formanek who published a description of it in 1895 and called it C. *cinerea*. This name had to be dropped when it was again collected and described in 1897 by Dorfler, as it had already been used for a quite different plant. It was not found again until 1917, then just inside the Yugoslavian border. It had to wait until 1929 to be introduced to cultivation by Dr Giuseppi who found it in the Nidje Planina. Despite its restricted distribution and distinct appearance, C. *formanekiana* is not temperamental. Placed in a reasonably sheltered position, it will produce flowers over a long period. It is a beautiful plant which is easy to grow. It is monocarpic.

Seed is set plentifully, as is the general rule with biennial and monocarpic campanulas (it is sometimes the third year before it flowers), and if this is collected will germinate well - and if it is not collected replacement plants will be thick around the parent plant before winter sets in, and these may be thinned out or potted up without difficulty.

We have had the experience also documented elsewhere of finding a young rosette of this plant quite eaten away overnight by a snail, leaving only a barren stump; this has later produced a mass of new branches like a pollarded tree, and the plant has subsequently flowered for three years running. We do not, however, recommend this as a standard method of cultivation! Positively speaking, it is a lime-lover with a particular affinity for tufa in cultivation.

Campanula formanekiana has been successfully grown as a house plant in Denmark; kept in a pot indoors, where its normal bee-pollination is denied it, flowering continues for several months. The plant was given an AM in 1931, and is well described and depicted in the *Botanical Magazine* at t. 9436 (1936).

Synonym: *C. cinerea* Formanek.

C. FRAGILIS Cyr.

10cm x 15cm • Pale blue • June

'The unbranched stems are heaped and piled with beautiful ample open starry cups of blue',(3) says Farrer, adding that it is far too rarely seen. The reason is that it is hard to place. It is, in fact, probably best in a hanging basket, tumbling over a warm wall or the bench of an alpine house. The problems of cultivation are not so much hardiness, but the length of the easily broken stems. *Fragilis* does really mean 'fragile' rather than tender. Under glass it requires little attention, and it repays with charming pale flowers and an elegant shape.

The rootstock is woody, and the stems arise from the base. These bear shiny, almost fleshy, dark green leaves, rather like a celandine. They are rounded heart-shaped, approximately 1cm, and regularly notched. The lower leaves have very long petioles, the upper ones less so.

Like its near relative, *C. isophylla*, the flowers are a large, 2cm open bell, with a prominent style which extends beyond the petals. These are a delicate blue with a lighter centre. The narrowly pointed calyx segments are almost as long as the petals. This is one distinguishing point between it and *C. isophylla*, the other being the glossy hairless leaves, which are also generally smaller and of darker colour than its relative. This said, there is also in circulation a plant described as *C. fragilis* 'Hirsuta' which, as the name suggests, is covered in all its parts with copious silvery bristles and which, incidentally, should be propagated vegetatively, as seed frequently produces varying intermediate types. *C. fragilis* grows on limestone rocks in central and southern Italy.

Division of the woody rootstock is difficult, and so spring cuttings or seed are the best means of propagation.

C. fragilis subsp. *cavolinii* which is also in cultivation is in effect a miniature version of the type; the recumbent stems are shorter, the flowers smaller and less star-shaped. This variant, which comes from the central mountains of Italy, forms a tighter cushion than the type and looks well cultivated in a pot as well as on a rock garden.

Synonym: *C. barrelieri* Prest.

C. GARGANICA Ten.   AGM

12cm x 20cm • Blue • July/Sept

Cushion-forming evergreen tufts of small, glabrous, bright green and finely toothed heart-shaped leaves and bright blue stars held to the sun on short, fine stems and pedicels.

C. g. 'Blue Diamond'

Resembles the type in habit and size, but has a paler base to the corolla, which in an open flower appears as a sort of pale blue, five-sided diamond.

C. garganica ssp. cephallenica

Comes from the island of Kephalonia off the Western Greek coast. It has less shiny leaves, is larger in all its parts, a robust plant, and unfailingly hardy in spite of its southern origins. Flowers are pale grey-blue stars.

C. g. 'Dickson's Gold'

Of similar habit and size to the type, with clear pale blue flowers contrasting with the distinctly gold leaves in summer sun. This is a very appealing plant, generally slower-growing, but quite as robust and long-lived if grown in its preferred scree conditions. From Mr Dickson, of Ponteland, near Newcastle.

C. g. 'Hirsuta'

A grey-hairy form, with the same abundant flowering stems; and with dusky blue flowers. This sets seed abundantly, but in our experience the progeny are often intermediate in hairiness. Propagation of the hairy form must be from cuttings in spring.

C. g. 'W.H. Paine'   AGM

Originated in Tully, Co. Kildare, Ireland. It has a striking white base to the rich violet corolla.

C. 'G.F. WILSON' AGM
10cm • Violet-blue • July/Aug

This is *C. pulla* x *C. carpatica* subsp. *turbinata*. Slowly spreading tufts of gently scalloped and bluntly pointed ovate leaves arise from underground runners. These leaves are of the slightly yellowish colouring which is often associated with hybridity; as originally described in the literature, there were two forms of this cross – one considerably more yellow than the other and not apparently common today, if in cultivation at all. It was said to be by far the less robust of the two. From each tuft of leaves arise sparsely leafy stems bearing similar leaves and topped by semi-pendent bold bells of a deep violet-blue. This is a most attractive plant, and further increases in value because of its later flowering, which is at its height in July and to the end of August, even into September.

C. GLOMERATA L.
To 75cm x 30cm • Purple, White • June/Sept

This is a popular and readily available border plant, variable but sturdily perennial; it is one of the few campanulas indigenous to Great Britain, and is found throughout Europe and Asia.

    C. glomerata is clump-forming, and the basal leaves, usually longish, heart-shaped on stalks, and usually withered at flowering time, throw up stiff stems between eight and 75cm high. The stem leaves are narrower, shorter stalked and even clasping the stems, especially near the apex. They bear clusters of flowers in the axils, and the

Campanula garganica 'Blue Diamond'

Campanula garganica 'Dickson's Gold'

stem terminates with a similar dense cluster. The flowers, which tend to lose their individuality in the cluster ('glomerata'), are bell-shaped, upright and up to 45cm long. The calyx lobes are lance-shaped half the length of the petals and without any appendages. The three-part style is not exserted beyond the petals.

The rootstock, creeping naturally but not dangerously so except in some light soils, is easily divided. Margery Fish calls it by its country name 'Peel of Bells' and says:

It would, I think, be elevated to a most distinguished position in the plant world if it did not run so badly... yet when it flowers I cannot help thinking what a very handsome plant it is. I do not know many flowers in that rich deep blue, and the clustered heads, on stout stems are most welcome in early summer... I also like the white flowered form var. Alba. White flowers, especially those that do not need staking, are always most useful in the garden. [4]

Agreed!

This type of plant is excessively leafy, but selected cultivars, as follows, are very attractive, and make good border plants, growing equally well in scree or crevice..

C. g. var *acaulis*

A very short-stemmed variant, often 8cm in height. Intermediate forms are common.

C. g. var. *alba*

White, single flowers, offered also under various but not always distinctive names, such as:

C. g. 'Alba Nana'

A very short-stemmed plant, usually with abundant white flowers. 'Nana Alba' is, of course, the same thing !

C. g. 'Caroline'

This is a shortish plant with amethyst-coloured flowers, but does not appear robust. A wild pink form, which may be the same, has been noted on Salisbury Plain [5] , and similar sports are thrown very occasionally in gardens.

C. g. var *dahurica*
75cm

From southeast Siberia, and one of the best. Tall, strong stems with flower heads of violet blue. (AM 1965.)

C. g. 'Joan Elliott' (Elliott)
30cm

Rich deep violet clusters; early flowering, and a plant that stands well.

C. g. 'Purple Pixie' (Bloom)
20cm

Violet-purple; dwarf, with good stem clusters; later flowering.

C. g. 'Schneekrone' ('Crown of Snow')
50cm

A good tall white form with copious clusters in all leaf axils, originating in Germany.

Campanula glomerata 'Schneekrone'

Campanula glomerata 'Superba' at Hidcote

C. g. 'Superba'

Violet-purple, and one of the best coloured; tall, 60cm, beautiful, but one of the more invasive (AM 1954). This is probably the same as var. *dahurica* in practice. Suspect any plant that needs 'Superba' for sales purposes.

C. g. 'White Barn' (Chatto)

Intermediate in size; forms a good clump. Contradictorily, the abundant flowers are blue.

Double forms have been described, but as the flower heads are already clustered any effect is largely lost. Most may be cut back after flowering, when they will repeat, if less strongly.

Synonyms: *C. eo-cervicaria* Nab.; *C. maleevii* Fedorov; *C. aggregata* Willd.; *C. cephalotes* Fisch.

C. GROSSEKII Heuffel

80cm x 30cm • Violet • July/Sept

This plant ran into trouble when Farrer got hold of its name. Of his two great loves – words and plants – the former got the best of him, and the latter gained its reputation – as gross. Grossek was in fact an amateur botanist, and, like the plant, of Hungarian origin.

From an evergreen rosette of coarse, heart-shaped leaves on long stems, bristly stems rise bearing similar but stemless leaves. The stem is branched and bears short-stemmed violet-blue funnel-shaped flowers, either solitary or in small clusters. They are about 3cm long, and have a hairy calyx which has pointed lobes, with slightly shorter, curved and pointed appendages. The pollen is characteristically bright yellow.

Like C. *trachelium*, which it resembles, it is a plant of stony woodland places, and so looks at its best in the wild or woodland garden, and certainly in a well-drained and poorer soil.

Seed is plentifully set, and this is the best source of the plant in the first place, and of its subsequent increase. Were the

Campanula 'Hallii'

plant more widely cultivated, no doubt white versions would crop up, and even perhaps doubles, which would make it more interesting. It can be up to 1m (three foot) in height in cultivation, and will take quite heavy shade.

C. 'HALLII'
10cm • White • July

This is a cross between C. *cochleariifolia* and, probably, C. *portenschlagiana*, it but betrays very little if any of the latter's influence, though upon close examination it can be seen that the glossy pale green leaves are intermediate between those of the two parents. The white flowers are borne singly on the 10cm stem. In effect, there is little to differentiate it from a tallish-stemmed white C. *cochlearifolia*. It was introduced in the 1920s by Alva Hall of Harrogate, and obtained an AM in 1923.

C. 'HAYLODGENSIS'
15cm x 10cm • Powder blue • August

This is a cross between C. *carpatica* and C. *cochleariifolia*, raised by Mr Augustine-Henry at Hay Lodge, near Edinburgh in 1885.

Originally, this campanula was a single-flowered plant, with the habit largely of the seed parent, C. *carpatica*, but showing the influence of the pollen parent in the erect openness of the cup-shaped bells. We could not positively assert that this single form is still in cultivation as originally known, though it would, of course, be easy enough

to repeat - and no doubt has been. However, the flower now well known under this name is its powder blue double seedling. The plant is slowly mat-forming, and because it is totally deciduous its robustness and hardiness have been queried, whereas it has perhaps fallen victim to an enthusiastic hoe. It succeeds in a well-drained position, like most of its kin.

A rosette of semi-folded, toothed ovate leaves 1cm long gives rise to ascending stems clothed sparsely with 15mm lanceolate leaves, the lower with petioles, and racemes of powder blue double flowers (in fact there are four whorls of petals) about 15mm across, with slightly flared petals; the tiny pointed calyx lobes have no appendages. The flower of this plant is larger and more open than that of 'Elizabeth Oliver', and they are borne on taller, 12-15mm stems. The leaves are also larger.

A white seedling of this plant is referred to under C. 'Warley White.

C. INCURVA Moretti
15cm x 20cm • Violet, White • June/ Sept

C. *incurva* comes from Greece and certain Aegean islands, and, although biennial or monocarpic, is both easy and hardy, and is well worth growing. The basal rosette, from a stout taproot, is of very characteristic pale green, with long-stalked, heart-shaped to triangular leaves. A number of hairy, slightly branching stems curve out and upwards ('incurva') bearing gradually smaller leaves which become

Campanula 'Haylodgensis'

stalkless towards the apex. The flowers are
very pale lilac or blue in lax panicles each
5cm long and bulbously bell-shaped. The
calyx has spreading triangular lobes and
short roundish appendages. The three-part
style does not project beyond the lobes of
the corolla.

Seed is large, flat and brown. It is set
copiously in the garden, and forms, of
course, the only means of propagation. We
have found germination rates to be good
and the plant self-sows copiously where it
is at its happiest; that is, in circumstances
close to those of its native haunts in the
Greek sun and on hard limestone. On the
wet clay of an unimproved border it
coarsens to show disapproval, but it will
still flower, and we have seen it survive cold
wet winters of frosty (down to -16°C)
weather. A slightly raised bed with plenty
of grit and some lime will show C. *incurva*
at its best.

An *alba* form is described, but as the
type is in any case very pale, this is not
particularly distinguished. The finest form
in our experience is pale lilac with slightly
deeper lilac edgings to the petals, but with
seedlings this is pure pot luck. Seed is quite
frequently offered in the exchanges of the
specialist societies (see p. 170). We think
this plant well worthwhile; so evidently did
the Royal Botanic Gardens, Kew, when they
exhibited it in 1937 and gained an AM.

Synonym: *C. leutweinii* Heldreich

C. ISOPHYLLA Moretti   AGM
15cm x 45cm • Violet, White • June/Sept

This is the easy-going plant of cottage
window-sills and hanging baskets. Even
neglect does not disturb its long and
brilliant flowering in late summer, and it
will continue to flower in winter in a
conservatory.

The rootstock becomes woody, but the
stems are soft and carry broadly oval
almost rounded leaves with a heart-shaped
base. They are mid-green, long-stalked and
with toothed edges. All the plant's leaves
are roughly the same shape and size; they
do not get narrower higher up the stem as
in many campanulas – hence the specific
name ('isophylla'). Most forms are hairless,
but some are very slightly hairy. The large
round starry flowers are held erect in loose
clusters. The calyx tube is short and so the
three-part style protrudes dramatically. The
calyx itself is about half the length of the
corolla, triangular and pointed.

This trouble-free plant can be
propagated by spring cuttings or from seed,
though the seed crop will be meagre. It
often survives outside; Margery Fish grew
it outside successfully in Somerset, but as it
is endemic to cliffs overlooking the Gulf of
Genoa in Italy, it dislikes too much winter
damp, and cold winds can break the soft
stems, but in cultivation it is surprisingly
hardy.

C. i. 'Alba'   AGM
This is a lovely white form, which received
an FCC in 1888. We have seen this in a
remote Turkish village, grown in an oil can

Campanula isophylla 'Alba'

and shaded from the sun by a tarpaulin. Fred Streeter, the much-loved BBC *Gardeners' Question Time* personality of the 1950s, recalled it. 'I well remember having to get up in the night to water this plant because my mother was afraid the campanula would be dry before morning, and would suffer. Oh, I didn't mind – but it made me careful to see it did not happen again. That's the way to teach you gardening!' [6] It is therefore thirsty!

C. i. 'Balchiniana' (erroneously C. i. 'Mayi')
Frequently cultivated in its variegated form, this plant is a hybrid between *C. isophylla* 'Alba' (pollen parent) and *C. fragilis* (seed parent). A plant was given to Messrs Balchin, who took cuttings, one of which threw a variegated shoot, from which a rooted plant gained an AM in 1896. [7] It is softly hairy, with broadly oval to heart-shaped leaves. The youngest leaves are often pink-tipped, and the cream

variegation comes and goes. The plant can sometimes appear to have lost its variegation completely, but then new shoots will be produced with a cream edge. There is a form in cultivation with a broad cream variegation, which appears more stable. The flowers are pale blue.

C. I. 'Mayi'   AGM

(This is probably to be credited to 'Balchinina').

Shown by Mr H. B. May, of Edmonton, London in 1899. [8] This was a good form of C. isophylla with showy heliotrope-grey flowers, darker towards the tips. Contemporary descriptions do not mention any variegation on the foliage. It received an AM in 1899 but is probably no longer in cultivation. The name has now become erroneously applied to C. i. 'Balchiniana'.

C. I. 'Flore Plena'

This is not commonly found. The flowers are smaller but with multiple corollas in copious hanging bunches of bright blue. It is a vigorous plant which replaces these hanging bunches as they mature with a further set, and then repeatedly over a season. We strongly suspect that it is in fact a hybrid, possibly with one of the Balkan species. In a hanging basket it is exceptional.

C. 'JOE ELLIOTT'   AGM
3cm x 8cm • Violet • May-June

This is a hybrid between C. raineri and C. morettiana, selected at the nursery of Joe

Elliott in the Cotswolds. Its habit is intermediate between the parents, with small roundish dark green leaves from a creeping rootstock, and large upright violet bells. It is probably easier to cultivate than either parent, but remains a plant for the specialist alpine grower, and is best in a pot in the alpine house.

C. 'JOHN INNES'
15cm x 70cm • Violet • July

This is an unlikely cross between Campanula carpatica as the seed parent and C. versicolor as the pollen parent. As soon as one sees it the parentage is indeed evident, for it appears what it is, a longer, prostrate-stemmed form of C. carpatica with versicolor flowers. A tuft of long pointed, heart-shaped leaves, intermediate between those of the parent plants, throws out radiating runners 30cm or more long, slightly branched and, typically, turning up a the ends. From July onwards these bear a succession of upturned star-shaped bells some 3cm across, of a rich lilac or lavender with violet centres. These flowers, with their deeply cut and sharply pointed centres, have a lightness not seen in the carpatica tribe generally.

This plant is long-lasting and does well in any normal soil, looking particularly good at the base of the larger rock-garden. It is sometimes found under the name C. x innesii; but under nomenclature rules, 'John Innes' seems more appropriate. Crook in his monograph referred to C. innesii, and gave the parents as carpatica and *pyramidalis*, but it is thought that this is a slip on his part, as his notes and cuttings from past literature refer to *carpatica* and *versicolor*.

The original plant was a hand-pollinated hybrid made at the John Innes Institute when it was at Merton in Surrey. We have not been able to obtain further details.

C. KEMULARIAE Fomin
30cm • Blue • July

This plant, endemic to the Caucasus, in cultivation falls between the border and the rock garden; but, it can make a neat front row to the former, especially if it is tumbling over a paved edge.

Allied to *C. raddeana*, it is a perennial with a thick creeping rhizome. The basal cluster of leaves are oval with a heart-shaped base. They are sharp pointed, strongly doubly-toothed, and on stalks longer than the blade. The stems are some 30cm long, and much branched, bearing oval leaves incised at the base and pointed at the tip on diminishing stalks. The flowers are on long pedicels, and of a sometimes rather dullish blue colour – this seems to depend on the type of soil in which they are grown. The natural habitat is on limestone in open forest, and this may give a clue to producing a better plant. The corolla is a wide bell shape, with a style which extends beyond the petals and bears orange pollen. The calyx teeth are smooth, triangular, and with no appendages.

C. kemulariae will bear its flowers more

proudly if grown in soil which is not too rich. It is also recommended for growing on a wall.

C. kemulariae alba, the white form, is a fine little plant, vigorous and effective in a pot or hanging basket, with its myriad of flowers in clusters at the end of the branches reminiscent of grapes.

C. 'KENT BELLE'
80cm x 30cm • Violet • July

This is a recent introduction which occurred spontaneously in the nursery garden of Elizabeth Strangman in the English county of Kent. It is a vigorous hybrid between *C. takesimana* and *C. latifolia*, reminiscent of and parallel to that between *C. punctata* and *C. latifolia*, and a splendid and popular plant.

The basal leaves and stem leaves, the latter on diminishing petioles up the stout stem, are all a toothed heart-shape; up to eight rich violet blue flowers in a loose cluster are of a thick tubular bell-shape. The calyx lobes are long triangular, and there are no appendages.

The creeping rootstock forms a mat in a moist semi-shaded soil, throwing up stems as it goes, and these may be used for propagation. After flowering it may be cut to a few inches in height, when fresh flowering stems will readily arise until autumn.

C. KOLENATIANA Mey.
40cm x 20cm • Blue • July

This is another Caucasian and close to C.

Campanula 'Kent Belle'

Campanula kolenatiana

sarmatica. A thick root gives rise to a tuft of longish-petioled leaves, ovate, toothed and with heart-shaped base. Several stems bear gradually smaller sessile leaves, and a one-sided raceme of drooping violet blue bells with flared lobes on short pedicels, often with bracts. The flowers are slightly hairy within, the calyx smooth and with triangular appendages, and the style is the same length as the corolla or only slightly exserted. Both leaves and flowers have a slight greyish effect, though this is less than in *C. sarmatica*. Crook writes of it as biennial, but we find it perennial, and though it has no strong personality it is a neat little plant, especially grown several to a container.

Campanula lactiflora in border at Beth Chatto's garden

C. LACTIFLORA Bieb.

To 150cm x 60cm • Blue, Pink, White • July/Sept

When Farrer, Crook and Graham Stuart Thomas use terms like 'superb', 'one of the finest...' and 'one of the best dozen border plants', one stops to ponder ....

The rootstock is branched and fleshy, becoming woody with age. The oval leaves, usually mid-green, are thin in texture, toothed and with little if any petioles. The strong erect stems have abundant oblong leaves, and branch to produce a broad leafy panicle of erect, individually modest-sized flowers, 2cm long, but in sufficient numbers to form a striking head. The individual flower is widely bell-shaped, milky blue ('half-fat, chain-store, pasteurised Friesian')[9] shading to a white centre. The flaring petals of the bell are divided to half-way down, and have a short style within them. The calyx lobes are largish, but have no appendages.

The plant will do well in the open sunny border, but really prefers partial shade, and must have a moisture-retentive soil to perform well. Because of its profuse seeding (E. A. Bowles spoke of its becoming a weed at Myddleton House, and we find no difficulty in agreeing with him), it should be dead-headed. Bowles also recommended cutting it back to just below the lowest flowers. This can increase the flowering period for a total of up to ten or 12 weeks in all, which is, by any measure, good value for money. The plant does not usually need staking, despite its height, unless it is exposed to strong winds.

As indicated, seed is set, but is not easily saved, as the bearing and habit of the plant ensure that all seed is scattered just ten minutes before attempted collection! Self-sown seedlings may be moved with some success whilst very small, but this plant does not like being moved without sulking for a while, and the eventual plants obtained in this way are never quite as good as the original. If potted up as a seedling, we have found it best over-potted until planting out, to give minimum disturbance to the root system. Named varieties may be increased by cuttings taken from new growth in spring. It is difficult to divide the thick tenacious roots, and the plants object to it. Robin Lane Fox had a tip for seed collection: 'Oddly, it sets ripe seed within a month of flowering and can be raised by the hundred if you sow it quickly in the same month.'[10]

This is a native of the Caucasus, but has become naturalised in many areas, including Scotland.

C. l. 'Alba'   AGM

A white variant; the whole flower, including the eye should be a pure white as opposed to light grey.

C. l. 'Blue Cross' (Bressingham)

A recent introduction which is an average and undistinguishable mid-blue.

C. l. Ssp. celtidifolia

From Siberia, has smaller but bluer flowers. Infrequently found; only from wild collected seed.

Campanula lactiflora 'Loddon Anna'

C. l. 'Coerulea'
A deeper, China blue (AM 1901).

C. l. 'Loddon Anna'   AGM
A fine flesh-pink sport raised in Carlile's nursery in Reading. It does not come true from seed (AM 1952).

C. l. 'Pouffe' (Bloom)
A mid-blue sport, long-flowering, and less than 30cm tall (AM 1967).

C. l. 'Prichard's Variety'   AGM
Very good choice. Dark purple bells, 75cm. From Prichard's nursery (AM 1964). Unfortunately, the name is often taken in vain for anything which is not the original milky blue. *Caveat emptor*. RHS Colour Chart 87A, with a slightly lighter centre, is the only passport to the real thing.

C. l. 'White Pouffe'
Another aptly named hummock, a white short-stemmed sport, with more vigour than the blue 'Pouffe'.

C. l. 'Superba'
AGM Large violet-blue flowers (AM 1969). There are records of this; though we have not seen it.

Synonyms: *C. biserrata* C. Koch; *C. celtidifolia* Boiss. & Huet.

C. LANATA Friv.
70cm • Cream • July/Aug

This really is as woolly as the name suggests; a fine, short-piled grey flannel on large heart-shaped, pointed leaves from long, equally hairy petioles. The stem is branched from the base, the branches often prostrate, and the upper forming a pyramidal inflorescence. The stem leaves are smaller but of similar shape to the lower, and on increasingly short petioles, while the upper are quite stalkless. In the leaf-axils, and on short pedicels, are held good-sized bearded 'Canterbury Bells' of palest cream or pink, hairy inside, which contrast well with the grey flannel of the leaves. The calyx is bulky, leafy, with triangular lobes, and long pointed appendages which turn back on themselves. The three-part style is shorter than the petals, and is sprinkled with a bright yellow pollen, which serves to help recognise the plant.

This is a handsome plant, but has the misfortune of being either biennial or monocarpic. Seed is, however, abundantly set, easily collected and will germinate well in the following spring if sown in late winter. Its woolliness does not give the sensitivity to winter wetness that would perhaps be expected, but a position protected from the extremes of sogginess which could otherwise afflict it will provide better plants and a more satisfied grower. *C. lanata* comes in nature from rocky clefts and cliffs of Bulgaria and Northern Greece, and also Yugoslavia. Being a high mountain plant it is hardy to considerable extremes of cold, so long as its roots are protected

Campanula latifolia 'Alba'

from too-often repeated freezing and thawing of a wet soil. In Cambridgeshire clay it does well in an open border which is reasonably well drained. Seed is, of course, the only way of acquiring and propagating *C. lanata* and this is usually offered by the specialist societies and one or two specialist growers.

Synonym: *C. velutina* Vel.

C. LATIFOLIA L.

To 100cm x 50cm • Blue, White • July

A dense mass of fleshy roots form a clump of oval to oblong leaves with a heart-shaped base. They are toothed, have a pointed tip and are on stalks of varying length. Firm, straight, upright and unbranched stems bear similar oval, stalkless leaves. Both leaf and stem are slightly hairy. Borne in the leaf-axils, and also in a terminal cluster, are the longish bell-shaped flowers, up to 6cm in length, and held either upright or pendent. In the type they are either light blue or pale lavender in colour. The calyx lobes are about half the length of the corolla and are without appendages.

This is a native of most of Europe, including the northern part of Britain and central Asia. It is absent from the Mediterranean area. It often inhabits woodland or lush meadows, and frequently on slightly acid soils, where it can be invasive. The cultivars, selected for colour, have the virtue or fault of being less rampant. They like a moist, humus-rich soil, and do best with some shade, though they will also grow well in full sun. C. *latifolia* makes a good border plant and, while the flowering period is not long, it makes an attractive show. As David Stuart and James Sutherland said in their book, *Plants from the Past*, 'its toughness in the face of competition and difficult conditions make it a most elegant plant for wild or woodland gardens. We found the white one among the nettles when we took over our 17th-century walled garden.' [11]

Propagation may be by division, most easily in spring; seed is plentifully set, and resultant seedlings will, of course, vary.

The following cultivars are well known:

C. l. 'Alba'

Single white; height variable, comes only partly true from seed.

C. l. 'Brantwood'

One of the best forms; deep violet blue, 90cm. Longer flowering and will repeat if dead-headed. From the English Lake District, and named after Ruskin's estate there. We have found that it sets a percentage of seed true to colour, and also divides very willingly.

C. l. eriocarpa

Said to be of Russian origin. Purple, 50cm. Less leafy, neat, and slow to spread. True only from wild-collected seed. Russian floras give it as a synonym of the type.

C. l. 'Gloaming' (Alan Bloom)

One of the most coveted, and a pleasing

Campanula latifolia 'Brantwood'

Campanula latifolia 'Gloaming' at Bressingham

smoky blue, 60cm. Not rampant enough for most tastes, and thus slow to propagate.

C. l. var *macrantha*

Large, deep blue flowers. Up to 100cm. Stem sparsely furnished with leafage because of the long internodes, hence tending to look bare and gaunt. Possibly a tetraploid.

C. l. var *macrantha alba*

White equivalent of the above.

C. l. 'Pallida' – a very pale blue.

C. l. 'Roger Wood' (Thelma Kay)

Campanula latiloba 'Hidcote Amethyst' and 'Highcliffe Variety' at Kiftsgate Court

Campanula latiloba 'Highcliffe' (see pg.98)

Campanula latiloba 'Hidcote Amethyst' at Hidcote (see pg.98)

Bicoloured, violet and white flowers on 100cm stems. Colourings will vary from its seed, especially if self-pollinated. It is an attractive new selection.

C. l. 'White Ladies' (Alan Bloom)

The purest virgin white, including the eye, with flowers large and long; a longer flowering period than some. 100cm, and well behaved, like a perfect lady.

Synonyms: *C. eriocarpa* Bieb. *C. macrantha* Bieb. *C. urticifolia* Bieb.

C. LATILOBA A. DC.
90cm x 30-45cm • Blue/White • July/Aug

This is very closely related to C. *persicifolia*, but to the gardener there are significant differences. C. *latiloba* is coarser and more robust, enabling it to display a strong sweep of colour in a large border - not a role for which C. *persicifolia* is so well suited. It is distinguished by its evergreen rosettes, individually similar to C. *persicifolia*, but larger and formed in clumps. The main distinctions are the quite stalkless and more open flowers of C. *latiloba* which are held on stiff rather thick angular stems, 10–15mm in diameter.

The long narrow leaves of the basal rosette are lance-shaped and toothed, with slightly winged petioles. They can reach up to 25cm long, with 16cm being more frequent. As usual, stem leaves are shorter and clasp the stem; they are hairless. Calyx lobes are broadly lance-shaped to triangular and hairless; they have no appendages. Flowers are 3-4cm and widely bell-shaped, quite stalkless and deep blue. The seed capsules open by three pores in the middle.

A patch of this plant forms a good ground cover, and whilst only the stronger rosettes form flowering stems, these do not normally need staking, and if blown over they tend to kink and turn upwards once more. Flowering is over a fairly long period, and the plants will repeat if cut down by half after the first flush. On the debit side, the stiff stems and stalkless flowers make the plant something of a clumsy country bumpkin compared with its elegant cousin C. *persicifolia*.

Margery Fish said, 'As a child this was the only campanula I knew and it was the whole family of campanulas to me. For years we hardly saw it except in tiny gardens, but it has once again come into its own in a better, deeper form as C. 'Highcliffe.' (sic) [12] and 'I would call C. *latiloba* a rambler; it certainly is with me... I am always finding stretches of its tufted green leaves in places where I certainly never planted it. It will send up its 18 inch (46cm) flower spikes in the most inauspicious places, the arid soil under hollies or poplars, the dry soil under walls, and I am sure would have a shot at covering any piece of waste soil. In these cases I find no difference in the energy of the blue and white forms.' [13]

Flora Europaea makes this plant C. *persicifolia* subsp. *sessiliflora* which is a meal of a name, and they have not convinced us. To the gardener there are such distinctive qualities that this diagnosis would never have occurred. We note, incidentally, that this plant is not a native of Western Europe, but of the Balkan peninsula, Turkey and the Caucasus. *The Flora of Turkey* refers to it as C. *latiloba*, while the Russians, who tend in general to be 'splitters', make it a subspecies of C. *persicifolia*.

The following are cultivated:

C. l. 'Alba' AGM
A particularly brilliant white, with a slim and more delicate shape which is rare but worth the search.

C. I. 'Hidcote Amethyst'   AGM

A lilac-pink mutation that was named after Hidcote Manor in Gloucestershire, where it is still grown, as at nearby Kiftsgate Court. The colour is a pale amethyst shading to a slightly deeper stripe at the centre of the petals and at their tips. Less coarse than the type and very desirable.

C. I. 'Highcliffe'   AGM

A rich lavender violet selected by Prichards, and a very strong grower.

C. I. 'Percy Piper'   AGM (Bloom)

Dwarfer than the type; again, a rich lavender violet, this has been reported to be a hybrid with *C. persicifolia* but evidence of this is hard to spot; in fact, it is hard to distinguish from 'Highcliffe'.

Synonyms: *C. persicifolia* spp. *sessiflora* (C. Koch) Velen; *C. sessiflora* C. Koch; *C. grandis* Fisch. & Meyer.

C. 'LYNCHMERE'

30cm x25cm • Dark blue • July/Aug

This miniature campanula won an Award of Merit in 1948, and Crook reported it as being showy and full of promise. In spite of this, it is not now in wide circulation. It is, however, obtainable, and invariably attracts the attention of every observer when it is in flower. It is thought to be a cross between *C. elatines* and *C. rotundifolia*, though *C. cochleariifolia* has also been given as a putative pollen parent. It forms a small 'bushlet' some 20-30cm in height of fine, branching stems with bright green oval leaves with blunt but regular teeth and a rounded rather than sharp tip. The branching is sparse, and the terminal flowers are pendent bells of a rich blue about 2cm in length and 1cm across, the slightly recurved petals of which are only shallowly divided. The colour is outstanding as revealing little of the red tone which is quite general in campanula flowers, making it one of the truest blues of all. This little plant is happy on the rock garden or in a pot, is long-lived, and, if given a haircut after flowering, will give a second crop of flowers until the frosts of autumn. Seed is not set, but though they will not be numerous, cuttings in autumn are as successful as those taken in spring; the former, perhaps with some bottom heat.

C. 'MARION FISHER'

5cm x 25cm • White • August

A delightful little plant which occurred in 1986 in a clump of C. 'Haylodgensis' in the garden of John Fisher in Cheltenham, subsequently introduced into circulation by his partner, John Anton-Smith. It is a pure white, falling in flower form and habit somewhere between C. 'Haylodgensis' and C. 'Elizabeth Oliver', all sharing, no doubt, similar parentage; it thrives in similar scree conditions. It makes an excellent sink or trough plant, and has proved soundly perennial. Like these two it has a multiple corolla, a white powder-puff about 12cm across.

Campanula 'Lynchmere' growing in tufa.

Campanula medium

C. MEDIUM L.

75-90cm x 30cm • Lilac, Blue, White • July/Aug

The well-known Canterbury Bells. A summer border of these large sturdy and free-flowering biennials is a dramatic sight, particularly as an adjunct to a rose garden.

In the first year plants form a rosette of elliptical leaves. They are roughly hairy, with rounded notches, and generally without stalks. In the second year the stout taproot produces an erect stem which is much branched, up to 90cm, with lance-shaped upper leaves. Flowers are lilac or white in wild plants, but in cultivation there are many shades of blue through to purple, mauve or rose. They are showy, more or less erect and wide at the base. The bells are about 6cm, oblong with stubby flaring lobes usually recurved at the rims. The calyx has large heart-shaped and reflexed appendages, and the style bears five stigmata.

C. *medium* is endemic to France and Italy at their Mediterranean borders, but is naturalised elsewhere in Europe. It is, for example, established on railway embankments in the Southeast and East Midlands of Britain, and extensively in Central Europe.

Sow seed in summer in a nursery bed, and sift silver sand over it. Prick out into rich soil, 20cm apart. Lift and plant out in the autumn. Alternatively pot up and grow in a conservatory where it is very effective for late spring.

In cultivation there are two different double forms, where the calyx becomes petal-like. In one this becomes a double bell, one inside the other, called cup-in-cup or hose-in-hose. In the other the calyx is spreading, and forms a saucer to the bell's cup.

Seed is available of a single-flowered strain of blue, dark rose, lilac, pink and white. Double-flowered strains are also offered in blue, pink and white, and in cup-and-saucer forms in the same colours and also lilac. Seed firms in Britain offer most of the above, and also a dwarf strain. It is a matter of individual choice. Robin Lane Fox wrote 'My family do not share my love of the double forms, especially in shades of ink purple, but you may agree with me in liking their gross vulgarity.' [14] In the 18th century there were striped blue and white Canterbury Bells, but these seem to have been lost.

C. *medium* has received many Awards of Merit over the years. C. *m.* 'Calycanthema' (the cup-and-saucer form)

was exhibited by Veitch and received its AM in 1889. C. *medium* 'Cup and Saucer' holds an AGM. In the same year Veitch also exhibited C. *m.* 'Flore Pleno', presumably a cup-in-cup which received an AM. There followed C. *m.* 'Flore Pleno Roucarmine' 1929, C. *m.* 'Meteor' 1915, C. *m.* 'Single White Improved' 1971 and C. *m.* 'White' 1929 from Webb and Dobbie. We must assume that they were all seed strains.

This easy biennial has rather fallen from favour. It is perhaps rather hairy and coarse, and its dead flowers hang on the plant, so that it benefits greatly from dead-heading. Its advantages, however, are a midsummer flowering (so that it does not leave the gap caused by removing spent wallflowers or sweet williams, for example) and the lovely soft shades which can be relied upon to produce a sea of colour whatever the weather. A large border could be interplanted with a dahlia like 'Coltness Gem' which would give a continuation of display.

Synonym: C. *speciosa* (Not C. *speciosa* Pourret)

C. MIRABILIS. Alb.
30cm x 45cm   Lilac, Blue   July/Aug

The student of etymology will recognise 'marvellous' in the specific name, and the plant, so little known today, is more than worthy of it. The *Flora of the USSR* says: 'A rare, very beautiful plant, cultivated since 1898.'

The Russian botanist Nicolas Albov

found just one plant of this campanula in the Caucasus; and brought it to the Boissier herbarium in Geneva for preservation. Henry Correvon later found among the dried material two capsules with ripe seed; this gave the first cultivated plants, a sample of which, shown in 1898, immediately won a First Class Certificate.

The large flat basal rosette is made up of smooth, glossy, dark green leaves, oblong (widest at the apex), with a long flanged petiole. The margins have rounded notches and are furnished with stiff transparent hairs which look like prickles – a feature which makes this campanula instantly recognisable even when quite tiny. Eventually a stiff pyramidal central stem develops with a few branches from the base, and these are clothed with alternate leaves similar to those of the rosette but wider at the base, and stalkless. Short branches arise from the leaf axils bearing up to four large, pale lilac flowers occasionally as much as 10cm across, but usually 7cm and of a good bell shape. The petal lobes are one-third the tube length, and the style does not project. Calyx lobes are broadly lance-shaped or triangular; the appendages are also triangular and as long as the calyx tube. The edges of the calyx lobes bear translucent prickles like those of the leaves. Albov's original plant bore more than 100 flowers.

Veitch wrote: 'This plant (in a pot) is grown in pebbles with very little soil, and we think this is the secret of success with this kind. The seed was sown three years ago.' [15] Crook is of the opinion, however,

that it will not give of its best grown in this way and needs a richer soil in a position such as a rock crevice, where the neck will be protected from damp. For ourselves, the best we have ever grown was self-sown in the sand-plunge of the alpine house – it was growing, therefore in pure and unfertilised sand! C. mirabilis loves lime and sun. It is very suitable for pot cultivation where, when well treated, it will make a grand show.

Propagation must be from seed, which is plentifully set. It may take three to four years to flower when, being monocarpic, it dies.

C. mirabilis is from Transcaucasia and has been described as a tertiary relict. Occurring as it does at the epicentre of the genus, closer study of the species, especially from an evolutionary point of view, might well produce interesting information on the genus as a whole.

C. 'MIST MAIDEN'
20cm • White • June/July

Although the origins of this are obscure, it is certainly well named. Brian Mathew, reporting its Award of Merit in the *Quarterly Bulletin of the Alpine Garden Society*, wrote of its being among the most graceful of the white-flowered campanulas. It was shown for its award in 1981 by Ingwersen, but its raiser is unknown, as is the exact parentage, though it is not hard to see the probability that C. rotundifolia and/or C. tommasiniana had a hand somewhere. Pure white pendulous or horizontal bells with flared mouths are held five or so to a fine wiry stem, making a well-grown plant seem very floriferous. Leaves at the base of the stems are oval to widely lance-shaped, about 1cm long on equally long, or longer petioles; the sparse stem leaves are narrow and the petioles become shorter.

This plant is suitable for rock-garden or pot cultivation, and in spite of its delicacy is thoroughly perennial. It spreads slowly by underground runners, and these may be used for propagation, preferably in spring as growth restarts.

C. MOLLIS L.
5cm × 25cm • Lavender • June/Sept

This rock-garden campanula comes from the south of Spain, but has close relations in neighbouring areas of North Africa. It has a somewhat confusing nomenclatural background, having borne the names of *C. malacitana* and *C. velutina*, which, added to the subspecific names accorded by the best of authorities, can leave one bewildered. *Flora Europaea* favours the name of *C. mollis* at least for the European species, and as this is, as far as we can say, by far the most common in cultivation, we hold to it.

This plant, from a thoroughly perennial rootstock, forms a rosette of small spoon-shaped leaves. From among these are thrown out a number of ground-hugging stems of about 20cm long, towards the end of which appear the flowers, upturned

funnel-shaped bells of pale lavender or lilac (the shade can vary considerably) on longish pedicels. The stem-leaves are round and stalkless. The corolla is split to half-way and the petals are flared to show a paler centre to the flower; the veins, however, are stained lilac of a stronger hue. The whole plant tends to be grey with short silky hairs. It obtained an AM in 1932.

C. m var. *gibraltarica*
A plant larger in all its parts; it appears to be more floriferous; and we can affirm that in our garden, in a landscaped 'Mediterranean house', it has been accustomed to show at least a couple of flowers in every month of the year. The flowers are 2cm long as grown by the authors; the corolla is pale without, but the inside is a deep rich lavender with a pale base. The style bears three stigmas which are much shorter than the corolla, reaching barely to the base of the clefts of the lobes, which themselves are not so reflexed as in the above type. Calyx lobes are long-pointed, with small triangular reflexed appendages. The deep violet staining of the petal lobe veins remains, but is not so outstanding against the deeper overall shade.

This is a rewarding plant to grow, but as the prostrate stems are very fragile, wind and rain are their constant enemy unless they are sheltered. As for most Mediterranean plants in the British climate or equivalent, sharp drainage is essential. The single rosette forbids division, but seed is usually set in the sheltered position recommended, and this offers the best propagation method; late winter sowing seems to give best results. When happy it will self-sow, and this is not uncommon in an undisturbed sand-plunge, whence it will transplant happily.

Synonyms: *C. malacitana* Herv. *C. velutina* Desf.

C. 'MOLLY PINSENT'

22cm • Violet-blue • July/Aug

This is a little-known and badly documented hybrid of not surprisingly unknown origin. A not-strongly spreading rootstock produces lax rosettes of crinkled heart-shaped finely pointed leaves which have a tendency to fold up from the midrib. They are longer than broad, and held on petioles about equal to their length. These leaves are irregularly and widely toothed, almost lobed in part. The sparingly branched stems, some 20-25cm in height, bear similar but sessile leaves, and, singly at their tips, violet-blue flowers of a good rounded bell-shape. The corolla lobes are divided to about one-third, and but slightly reflexed; when opened they are held horizontally. The calyx lobes are long and fine, without appendages.

The leaf suggest the almost inevitable *C. carpatica* parentage; more is unknown, and the only, brief, mention we have traced is in Alan Bloom's *Alpines for Your Garden*, 1980.

We have this little plant in cultivation in Cambridgeshire; it flourishes in a rock-garden or sink, is hardy, easy and trouble-free, and has survived many years planted in tufa in an exposed spot.

It may be noted that Cecil Pinsent was a garden designer in the 1920s, and there is a hybrid saxifrage 'Kathleen Pinsent', but we have no further details of the original naming.

C. 'NORMAN GROVE'

15cm • Blue • Summer

The origin of this hybrid is now uncertain, but *C. isophylla* and *C.* 'Stansfieldii' are given by Crook as the possible parents. If so, the habit more resembles that of the latter than the former. It is certainly a robust and long-lived perennial, and reasonably hardy in a well-drained soil. From a tuft, it spreads slowly into a mat of small triangular heart-shaped leaves from which stems ascend with few lance-shaped leaves and topped by semi-pendent cup-shaped bells of mid-blue, borne on longish pedicels.

Norman Grove, of Sutton Coldfield, was a campanula enthusiast who grew and showed a number of alpines before the outbreak of the First World War. C. 'Chastity' was shown by him and obtained an AM in 1916. This was a free-flowering seedling of C. 'Norman Grove'; a plant a little taller, to 25cm, bearing, as the name suggests, flowers of a pure white. Another of his awards plants is noted under C. 'Enchantress'. We have not been able to trace modern sources of either of these plants, but C. 'Norman Grove' is readily available.

C. OCHROLEUCA Kem. Nath.

30cm x 45cm • Creamy white • June-July

This species is by some considered a subspecies of *C. alliariifolia*. It occurs in Transcaucasia and is, as the name betrays, a creamy-white in colour, which in a good form is attractive. The chief difference botanically is that the style extends beyond the corolla, but in the garden this is a useful if homely ground cover plant for the larger rock-garden, forming a very dense, if floppy, mat or cushion of bright green heart-shaped leaves on long petioles, and bearing rich cream flowers on a one-sided raceme. It stands at 30cm in height before flopping, but this does not seem to spoil its effect, and it serves as appealing carpet.

Synonym: *C. alliariifolia* subsp. *ochroleuca*

C. PALLIDA Wall.

This is a biennial from the Himalayas which turns up in seedlists; it is not very effective.

C. pallida ssp. *tibetica* is not dissimilar from the type, and could almost be taken for a dwarf version of *C. cashmeriana*, if one needed such. Its virtue is that it is · perennial.

Synonym: *C. colorata* Wall.

C. 'PAMELA'

⌐ x 40cm • Violet/white bicoloured • Aug

one of the few intentional crosses a⌐⌐ ⌐ampanulas, and a great success. C. ei⌐ ⌐ parent was crossed with C. iso⌐ ⌐he result a prostrate plant ⌐trailing brittle stems bearing c⌐⌐ ⌐tar-shaped flowers some 4cm across, white with vivid violet shading at the outward centres of each petal. Calyx lobes are lanceolate and there are no appendages. Leaves are pale green, ovate-cordate and with large teeth.

The plant is hardy and long-lived, but sterile. Propagation must be by division, and the base, becoming woody, makes this difficult, and so the process becomes slow.

We mention this plant not because it is readily available, but because it presents possibilities of repeated hybridisation between suitable species. It won an AM in 1953.

C. PATULA L.

30cm x 20cm • Violet-blue, White • July

C. patula is one of only five British native campanulas, possibly a good reason for its inclusion in this book. Another good reason is Farrer's description in *The English Rock Garden* of it 'filling the alpine meadows with a tossing sea of hot lilac-lavender'. [16] We appreciate that Farrer's description gives a gardening impression which may not satisfy the scientific attitude of a botanist; His description is of a living, flourishing plant, whilst the botanist is satisfied with the more accurate dead parts

Campanula 'Pamela'

of the plant on a herbarium sheet –
divorced from its environment, natural or
horticultural.

This is a biennial with a fine, fibrous
root system, and whose leaves and stem are
scabrid (thin and dry), but they are very
many when well grown in the garden, and
the effect is of a tall, profuse and starry
harebell. The lower leaves are more or less
oblong, wider at the tip, their edges
notched. The base of the leaf becomes a
short stalk. Stem leaves are smaller,
narrower and stalkless, their margins less
notched. The flowering stems are branched
and spreading, their flowers often very
numerous and held erect. The lobes of the
corolla (½cm) are about as long as the tube,
which narrows at the base. The calyx teeth
are triangular and held erect. Differences in
the margins of the calyx teeth, more of
interest to the botanist than the gardener,
give the subspecies mentioned below. When
the seed capsule is produced it opens with
pores at the top. Again, Farrer's description
gives the best impression 'Its stem can
attain two or three feet (60-90cm), wirily
slight and slender in growth, set all up with
oval-toothed leafage, veiny and flimsyish;
then crowning the stems in a loose shower
are several, or many, wide, erect and
particularly full-rayed stars, or shallow
bells, of a luminous rose-purple, varying to
palest tones and a stainless white.' (16) The
"luminous rose-purple" in a good form is
most striking.

C. patula is a plant of shady woods and

hedge-banks, and was formerly found throughout England and Wales from Dorset and Kent to Shropshire and Durham. It is now local and uncommon, and principally confined to Severn and Wye valleys in the West, but occurs widely in central and northern Europe.

C. patula ssp. a. *abietina* var. *vajdae* Sometimes found referred to as *C. vajdae*, is a dwarf mountain form of *C. patula* subsp. *abietina*.

Flora Europaea gives the following subspecies occasionally found under the specific names:
C. p. subsp. *abietina* (Griseb.) Simonkai is described here under *C. abietina*.
C. p. subsp. *costae* (Willk.) Fedorov
C. p. subsp. *epigaea* (Janka) Hayek
C. p. subsp. *patula* - the type plant.

C. PERSICIFOLIA L.

90cm x 30cm • Lilac-blue • July/Aug

The peach-leaved bellflower is easily brushed past unnoticed in its native open woods, scrub, thickets or alpine meadows, but in the garden it is altogether larger and more beautiful. It is a refined and good-mannered plant and would probably be more treasured if it were rarer.

On the ground there is an evergreen rosette of hairless linear to lance-shaped leaves with slightly notched margins. Underground it forms a white fibrous root system. The wiry flower stems have a few smaller leaves, and from their axils the flowers appear on short pedicels. They open at the top in an elegant profusion of chubby bells. The flowers are 2-4cm across, with wide-open cup-shaped bells that are slightly nodding.

A native of Europe, Africa, North and West Asia, it was introduced into Britain in the 16th century. It is established in South Devon, Gloucestershire, Berkshire and possibly Yorkshire and Grampian on commons and open woodlands, and no doubt other spots as a garden escape.

Cultivation is quite easy, but not invariably reliable. The plants can be mauled by rough weather when flowering, and are not easy to stake. Some of the cultivated forms are susceptible to rust attack in late summer. For those so inclined, regular spraying as soon as rust is noticed is necessary. This has been dealt with in the chapter on cultivation etc. (See p. 33). Organic cultivation will protect from much of this weakening disfigurement. A moist rich soil over chalk is ideal but not essential. Like C. *pyramidalis* it can be grown in pots plunged in frames over winter, to be brought into a greenhouse for spring flowering. It will not thrive in a pot for long, but the more delicate cultivars are probably worth giving this treatment, for protection and conservation. Propagation by division is easy – it spreads, but does not really run, and seed germinates freely. It makes a good cut flower. Here the single forms are described first, and the double forms follow.

C. p. 'Alba'

A white form of the above. Different colour shades will be produced in any batch of seedling, though most will be lilac-blue.

C. p. 'Carillon'

A tall version of C. p. 'Alba', 106cm, introduced by Kelways. Flowers are 6cm wide x 4cm deep. Leaves 15cm long x 1cm wide and wider than most C. persicifolia. Resistant to rust.

C. p. 'Chettle Charm'

Introduced by Blooms this is about 60cm tall, and has cup shaped flowers. They are white, edged with a flush of pale china blue.

C. p. 'George Chiswell'

A recent introduction and a synonym for 'Chettle Charm'.

C. p. 'Grandiflora Alba'

The plant is large, 122cm x 60cm, with big flowers with more pointed corolla lobes than the type. A suspicion of purple gives softness to the white. It looks well from a distance, or grown as a specimen, since it is very floriferous. Grown in one or two gardens (AM 1890). Possibly the same as C. p. 'Backhousei'.

C. p. 'Snowdrift'

Single white. Recommended by Frances Perry and still grown in some gardens, and recently available from Blooms.

C. p. 'Telham Beauty'

This was a classic herbaceous border plant, forming a sturdy block of colour for many weeks. It is 90 x 60cm and vivid lilac-blue. A thicket of ample spikes carry 7cm-wide shallow lavender cups, in healthy profusion. Whereas C. persicifolia has 16 chromosomes, C. p. 'Telham Beauty has 32 and this larger size seems to relate to this doubling. (17) Its history is well documented. In 1705 something very like it was illustrated in the *Botanical Magazine*, as var. *maxima* from South Carolina. Then it vanished. During the First World War, F. D. Thurston, the gardener at Telham Court, Battle, in Sussex, reproduced it. In 1916 this plant 'Telham Beauty' received an AM. It was reported as having 10cm flowers, 12 to a spike, and was grown in pots for the conservatory. Its raiser recommended a light rich soil, division after flowering and a fungicide spray against rust. He also bred a pure white form. But in 1920 while moving, the plants were stuck for 14 days in a furniture van and died. A lot of inferior plants now masquerade under its name, and we doubt if it still exists. It was self-fertile.

C. p. 'Wedgwood'

This was raised from seed and exhibited by Watkins and Simpson in 1953 when it received an AM. The stiff erect stems are 112cm high and hold up to 50 flowers per stem, with 10-12 open at once. The flowers are 7cm across and 2cm deep, a violet-blue with conspicuous cream stamens. A plant named 'Wedgwood' is available from a few nurseries, but whether it is the same as the original cultivar is open to doubt.

Campanula persicifolia 'Chettle Charm'

C. p. 'White Queen'

Another strong white form which is available from several nurseries. *C. persicifolia* reproduces freely from seed, and white seedlings are common. Plants under this name may possibly not be the genuine article.

C. persicifolia var. planiflora

15cm   Lilac-blue or white   July/Aug

This is a rather smart little plant, but it just misses being first class. It is rather too stiff, and the flowers are disproportionately large.

The dark green leaves are thick, glossy and succulent-like, and have notched, slightly overlapping margins. The flowers are flattish, large, and held close to the stem. A curious feature is that, unlike other campanulas, the ovary appears to be superior, since it rises above the sepals. This is both misleading and disconcerting. The plant's history is also interesting. First illustrated in Dodart's *Histoire des Plantes* in 1676, it was then called '*Trachelium americanum minus flore caeruleo patulo*'! It survived that meal of a name, and Alphonse de Candolle [18] said that it was in many gardens and herbaria, and that the habitat was Arctic America. The Rev. Wolley Dod, of Malpas, challenged this in the *Gardener's Chronicle* of 1895: 'If this alleged species were lost, I would undertake to make it again in a few years by a selection of dwarf forms of *C. persicifolia*'. [19] His practical observations proved right in the 1920s, when the John Innes Institute did some breeding experiments. They

Campanula persicifolia var. *planiflora* 12cm high

showed it to be a Mendelian recessive. [20] Plants of *C. persicifolia*, being self-pollinated, produce *C. persicifolia planiflora* in proportion of 1 to 8. If *C. planiflora* is back-crossed with *C. persicifolia* then one *C. p. planiflora* to three *C. persicifolia* are produced. It breeds true from seed. Gardeners, however, clung to the Arctic America story for long thereafter.

It is usually grown in the rockery, but likes a little shade. Blue, pale blue, white, single and double forms have been noted, but the blue and white are now the only ones available. The white form received an AM in 1970 when exhibited by Valerie Finnis. More seedlings appear white than blue in our experience. Available from several nurseries.

Synonym: *C. nitida* Dodart

Campanula persicifolia Double forms

For convenience the double forms are listed together below. The *Botanical Magazine* of 1798 stated that double *C. persicifolia* had become so common as to usurp the place of single ones in the garden. We give details below of those we believe are still in cultivation. In the text W = width, D = depth of flower.

The 'doubles' can be exasperating plants. Sometimes they flower abundantly, but they can sulk too. Most increase quite well in the usual stoloniferous way. Large leaves in the basal rosette usually mean that the plant will flower, but if it does not it is worth lifting in late August, splitting the clumps and growing on in the vegetable garden for replanting in the border the following spring. Liquid feeding and mulching also help, and so does the spray for rust mentioned earlier. Many produce a little viable seed, which will produce some double-flowered seedlings, many of which are simply messy looking. It is only worth retaining plants which are

strong with a good clear outline.

C. p. 'Alba Coronata'
45cm • White • July/August

A dainty plant, whose flowers are usually two, sometimes three, rows of petals. The calyx has become enlarged and coloured white like the corolla. It is in effect a hose-in-hose type of flower, but cup-in-cup is more descriptive. Rosette leaves 11cm x 1½cm, flowers 5cm W x 3½cm D. Reintroduced by Mrs Joan Grout from an old garden in north Nottinghamshire. Sometimes sold as *C. p.* 'Alba Plena'.

C. p. 'Alba Flore Pleno'
60cm • White • July/Aug

Very double with many rows of petals. Possily the same as *C. p.* 'Gardenia' or *C. p.* 'Boule de Neige'. The flowers may decay in wet weather, but as a buttonhole they last very well.

C. p. 'Bennett's Blue'
75cm • Pale Blue • July/Aug

Introduced by Richard Blenkinship of Lincolnshire, a pale blue, very double flower on a strong stem - in effect a paler form of 'Pride of Exmouth'.

C. p. 'Boule de neige'
60cm • White • July/Aug

A very double flower with outer petals rolling back on themselves a little to give the impression of a ball. Not very strong and a martyr to rust. Rosette leaves 12cm x 1cm, flowers 5cm W x 3cm D. Received an AM in 1921. Unfortunately, 'Fleur de Neige

Campanula persicifolia 'Alba Coronata'

has been passed off as this.

C. p. 'Coronata'

46cm • China Blue • July/Aug

A semi-double cup-in-cup. The bell is square in section, and shallow, being 5cm W x 2½cm D. Calyx lobes linear and flat to the petals. Leaves linear 8cm.

C. p. 'Flore Pleno'

70cm • Lilac blue • July/Aug

A cup-in-cup with two rows of petals, and the centre filled with small petaloid stamens. The effect is of a small button rather like a rose or double primrose. Flowers 4cm W x 2½ cm D, leaves 13-15cm x 1cm. Though the flowers are small, they are plentiful. This name could refer to any double blue *C. persicifolia*, therefore plants offered may not be as good as the one described above, but it is worth taking a chance to acquire this desirable rose-like plant, which unfortunately has not been given a cultivar name.

Campanula persicifolia 'Bennett's Blue'

Campanula persicifolia 'Boule de Neige'

C. p. 'Fleur de Neige'   AGM
70cm • White • July/Aug

A very large tightly packed flower with approximately three rows of petals and petaloid stamens. The corolla lobes are pointed at the tips. It opens rather flat, as its dimensions of 5cm W x 3cm D imply.

Leaves 8cm x 1cm. It is grown in a few nurseries and gardens, but plants offered are not always correctly named. It is resistant to rust.

C. p. 'Frances' AM 1938
60cm • White/blue tinge • July

A recent rediscovery, this has approximately three rows of slightly wavy petals tinged with the faintest blue.

C. p. 'Frank Lawley'
60cm • Spode Blue • July

A medium-sized flower on fine stems with about three rows of wavy petals.

C. p. 'Gawen'
45cm • White • July

A semi-double cup-and-saucer, pure white and although quite short in stature, a vigorous plant. It was rediscovered in a derelict garden in Derbyshire, and is now available from one or two nurseries. Leaves are dark green. Flowers are 4cm W x 3½cm D, leaves 11cm x ½cm. See also 'Per Gawen' and 'Hampstead White'.

C. p. 'Hampstead White'
70cm • White, Green veining • July/Aug

A semi-double cup-and-saucer, rather like a distinguished Canterbury Bell. The veins on the backs of the petals and their tips are sometimes tinged with green. Available from several nurseries under different names. Flowers 5cm W x 3½cm D, leaves 13cm x ½cm. We can find no difference between this, 'Gawen' and 'Hetty' overleaf.

Campanula persicifolia 'Fleur de Neige'

C. p. 'Hetty'
70cm • White, Green • July/Aug

A semi-double cup-and-saucer. A vigorous and floriferous plant which has been re-introduced and named by Dr C. Hardwick in Surrey for his mother. It received a PC when exhibited by him at the RHS in 1985. Flowers 4½cm W x 4cm D, leaves 11cm x ½cm. See also above.

C. p. 'Moerheimii'
75cm • White • July

From the Dutch nursery. A good double white, similar to 'Fleur de Neige'.

C. p. 'Pike's Supremo'
70cm • Blue • July

Raised by Albert Pike at Impington, Cambridge, this plant has more than a hint of *C. latiloba* in its genes. The stems are thick and tall, and the dark blue flowers are held on very short stalks. They are large and semi-double, and the plant strong, and upright, if a little stiff in the border.

Campanula persicifolia 'Frank Lawley'

Campanula persicifolia 'Gawen' at Rise Top Cottage, Surrey

C. p. 'Pride of Exmouth'

60cm • Purple-blue • July/Aug

A semi-double cup-in-cup forming a dainty curved bell. This plant has been around for a long time, and therefore must be stronger than its thin stems and small stature suggest. Available from several nurseries, but some inferior plants are given this name in error. It stands up and repeat-flowers particularly well. Flowers 3cm W x 2cm.

C .p. 'Rearsby Belle'

80cm • Mid-blue • June/Aug

Bred in Leicestershire by Hazel Kaye, who took ten years to achieve it. A tall upright stem with large cup-and-saucer flowers. Bred from 'Hampstead White'.

C. p. 'Tinkerbell'

60cm • White

Another recent introduction by Hazel Kaye. Cup and saucer flowers, small but with a dainty outline.

C. p. 'Wortham Belle'

75cm • Blue • July

Introduced by Blooms, a rich blue cup-and-saucer in what we call shuttlecock form, with the outer petals turned sharply back to the stem.

Where are they now?

The following is a list of *C. persicifolia* names which have been mentioned in gardening literature, but which seem to be no longer in cultivation. Most date from the 1920s, but some are earlier. It is our view that some of these old forms will re-occur naturally from seed.

'Backhousei' S W 1883
'Beechwood' S B
'Blue bell' S deep B
'Blue Bird' S B
'Coupe d'Azure' D B
'Daisy Hill' B
'Delft Blue' D B
'Essie' S B 1953
'Everest' S B

'Fairmile' 1949
'Fairy Queen' S B/Grey 1927
'Gardenia' D W 1949
'Humosa' D B
'La Fée' S W
'Lavender Queen' B S
'Marion Knocks' 1955
'Misty Morn' D B
'Pfitzeri' D B
'Princess Royal' 1935
'Ruth Lansdell' 1959
'Shirley' D B AM 1925
'Spetchley' S W AM 1921
'The Crescent' S W
'The King' D B AM 1926
'Veneta' D B
'Verdun' D B 1926
'William Laurenson' S B AM 1901

Campanula persicifolia 'Hetty' and 'Hampstead White'

'Windsor Bell' D 1950
'Wirrall Belle' D B 1949

D = double, S = single, B = blue, W = white, AM = Award of Merit.

Synonyms: *C. crystallocalyx* (Adamovic); *C. persicifolia* subsp. *pyremaica* from the Pyrenees (*C. pyrenaica*); *C. persicifolia* subsp. *sessiflora*, syn. *C. latiloba*, and so treated here.

C. PORTENSCHLAGIANA
Schultes   AGM
25cm • Blue • June/Aug

This is the former *C. muralis*, a name which gives a hint to its best and most natural use, which is for mural decoration. It is one of the menaces among campanulas, albeit a modest one, in that, not content with the long questing stems reaching out to cover the ground, it has more reaching out below the surface of the soil in quest of fresh territory.

A fairly fleshy rootstock puts up a rosette or several rosettes of tiny heart-shaped leaves on very long stalks. These can grow up to about 5cm across; they are heavily toothed, often multiply so, and the margins are usually wavy at full size. The leaf-tip is rounded. Stems up to 40cm long are thrown out from the stock. These bear similar but smaller stalkless leaves, from whose axils further branches carry a number of flowers on short side stems. The flowers are funnel-shaped bells cleft into lobes about one-half their length, and these lobes are flexed outward at about 45°. The style is a little shorter than the petals, and bears three stigmas. The calyx lobes are small and fine-pointed, without appendages.

The colour of the flower is a uniform deep lavender. A selected form, from the Continent and known as 'Resholdt's Variety' is larger in all its parts, particularly the flowers, but these are vivid but paler in colour. A 'Major' variant is also offered where the flowers are larger. 'Lieselotte' is a continental selection which we have not seen.

This campanula does not need a rich soil, although it will do all too well in one. It will grow in crevices in the top or side of a wall ('muralis') with happy effect. Although the runners do quest far, in a more open situation they are not at all hard to control by just pulling them out; only in a neglected situation will they spread menacingly!

Synonym: *C. muralis* Portenschl.

C. POSCHARSKYANA Degen.
25cm • Various • June/Sept

Although this resembles *C. portenschlagiana* in many respects, the most immediate obvious difference is the shape of the flowers, which here are star-shaped. It is not quite such a coarse plant and the leaves are shorter stalked and smaller. On close examination the following differences also appear: leaves with slightly more pointed tips; toothing finer; stems covered, albeit sparsely, with fine bristles and considerably longer than

Campanula portenschlagiana

those of *C. portenschlagiana*, the most immediately noticeable difference.

The flowers, as we have said, are quite distinct. Here they are cleft to three-quarters or even four-fifths the petal length, and the resulting lobes are widely reflexed to give a flat star-shape. In the experience of some this plant, in the forms mentioned below, is less of an invasive creeper than *C. portenschlagiana*.

Side rosettes or short runners, with or without roots, may be taken for propagation as the plants resume growth in spring. These will all flower quite early in the campanula season, and if shorn after blooming will crop again right into and even through the frosts. They look particularly effective growing scandently against a wall. An AM was awarded in 1933.

C. p. 'Blauranke'

This is a German selection, the flower being deep violet blue with a clear white centre.

Campanula poscharskyana on a frosty morning at
Cambridge University Botanic Garden

Campanula poscharskyana 'Blauranke'

Campanula poscharskyana 'Lisduggan'

C. p 'E. H. Frost'

A milky-white which shows itself off especially well in a sink or trough, or on the edge of a raised bed, where it will tumble over. It may also be met as *C. p.* 'Albiflora'.

C. p. 'Glandore'

This is a tight bun, much less spreading. Flowers are a deep blue-violet. We suggest it may be a hybrid with *C. garganica*.

C. p. 'Lilacina'

Not usually to be distinguished from the following, though it may not have the red stems. Possibly the name sounds more sophisticated.

C. p. 'Lisduggan'

Flowers of an attractive flesh pink; hardy as the type but not so strongly growing. Found in a garden in Co. Wicklow, Ireland, the original had reddish stems.

C. p. 'Stella'

A particularly bright blue, and the flowering stems can reach 40cm or more in a rich soil, which, incidentally, is not necessary. Good authority tells us that this is in fact a hybrid raised by Georg Arends, using *C. garganica* as the pollen parent. It would appear that two hybrids mentioned elsewhere are closely related, but with stronger growth still – C. 'E. K. Toogood' and C. 'Constellation'. These could well have the admixture of *C. isophylla* 'blood'.

Campanula poscharskyana 'Stella'

Campanula poscharskyana 'E. H. Frost'

Campanula poscharskyana 'Glandore'

Variegated forms have occurred, but have proved neither stable nor long lived.

C. PRIMULIFOLIA Brot.
90cm x 30cm • Blue • July/Aug

'This is a good plant which deserves to be better known than it is, for it is eminently handsome and quite hardy, and may be made a great ornament to our flower borders.' So said the *Botanical Magazine* in October 1855, and so, still, say we ! When Farrer dismissed it as summarily as he did, we wonder if actually he knew and grew it. *C. primulifolia* comes chiefly from Portugal, principally in the Algarve and Beira, and also from Spain. It grows in sandy, moist soil in the shade of rocks, and is usually biennial, though it can persist for a second season of blooming, especially if cut back low on the stem after flowering.

The basal rosette looks exactly – but exactly – like that of a vigorous cultivated primrose. Fresh hispid, angular and succulent stems arise from the root, branching only from the base and so forming a pyramidal shape to the plant. Stem leaves are similar to the basal ones, but narrow to a much shorter winged, primrose-like stalk, and they become stalkless toward the apex. Flowers are borne terminally and in the leaf axils in bunches of three to five on short pedicels. The lower flowers are noticeably broader than the upper ones, but all are good broad bells, white in bud and spreading at the mouth as much as 5cm across, and of a handsome purple-blue with a paler base, somewhat reminiscent of the Chimney Bellflower. Calyx segments are lance-shaped, backward curving and without appendages. The style is short and divides into three.

This, in spite of its Mediterranean origins, is hardy. Seed is now more readily available than it used to be, and germinates prolifically. Subsequent plants are relatively slow to establish, and we have lost many by allowing seedlings to dry out. If they are treated like the primulas they so closely resemble – kept moist and shaded – they will thrive. One of us successfully raises them on capillary matting, where, unless they are well labelled, they soon get confused with the primulas which share the same bench. Once planted out, preferably in a deep humus-rich soil with some sand (drainage still needs to be good), they need to be kept moist until well established.

This plant is figured in the *Bot. Mag.* at t. 4879 (as *C. primuliflora*).

Synonym: *C. trachelium* Brot. (Not *C. trachelium* L. of today).

C. peregrina L.
The *RHS Dictionary* incorrectly refers to these as synonymous. *C. peregrina* (awarded AM in 1903), although not known at present to be in cultivation, describes a plant from the opposite end of the Mediterranean, and found in Cyprus, Rhodes, Turkey, Syria and Palestine. It is closely related, and is also found in similar habitats – at streamsides or in damp pine forest. The most obvious difference is that

here the flowers are darker at their centres, with lighter lobes, whereas in *C. primulifolia* the 'eye' is lighter in colour. *C. peregrina* is also biennial in habit.

Synonym: *C. lanuginosa* Lam.

C. 'PSEUDORAINERI'

15cm x 15cm • Blue • July/Aug

Farrer brought this one up, and although he was curiously indecisive about the name, he seemed to think well enough of the plant. Anyone who has grown much *Campanula raineri*, and our old friend *C. carpatica*, within wooing distance, has experienced the disappointment of sowing the carefully gathered *C. raineri* seed, to find that it had been unfaithful. No matter; a fine plant results, and probably one that is easier to keep than the true, pure *C. raineri*, less attractive to slugs, able to freeze for days in a small pot without failing to make a comeback – in brief, a valuable plant. Of course, the lingering uncertainly of its murky ancestry will cast gloom and loss of esteem over the purist, but the fine plant for its own sake remains. Because it is no new-fangled invention, we here propose to fix the name of *C. 'Pseudoraineri'* for the issue of a union between *C. raineri* as the seed parent and *C. carpatica* subsp. *turbinata* as the provider of pollen. There will be some variation in this first filial generation, but really remarkably little.

A slowly creeping tufted plant – like both parents – produces small, round and slightly pointed heart-shaped leaves, between parents again, and sparsely leafy stems about 10-15cm in height, with open blue saucers some 3½–4½cm across, rich and long-lasting in bloom. The chief variation may well be in the hairiness of the plants – hence the overall greenness or greyness, and in the shape and carriage of the petals.

The best can, of course, be proliferated by division, or cuttings in spring if a quantity is desired; those of the Irish variety, partly rooted offsets, can usually be found in plenty.

C. PULLA L.

12cm • Deep blue • June

This is one of the darkest coloured campanulas; *pulla* meaning 'very dark'. It comes from the Alps of Styria in Austria – a rich area for alpine campanulas. It is one of the best known and is freely available. It forms a mat of rosettes, each of small round shiny leaves on short petioles, and from virtually every rosette a fine stem about 10cm high, with a few stemless round and pointed leaves, bears a single pendent well-rounded bell of a deep purple-blue. The mat extends slowly, and this plant is not by any means invasive; some would claim not enough so! It is ideal in a sink or trough, but seems to exhaust a pot rather rapidly and is not happy there. It is a lime-lover, not rapid to establish, and tends to flower itself to death if not frequently divided. It has been said to demand shade; others are equally sure it

requires a sunny spot; we cannot detect much difference in results, but are certain that it does not tolerate drying out. A moisture-retaining soil, with abundance of both grit and humus, and due attention to water requirements, are the secrets, it seems, of success with this beautiful little campanula.

Propagation is by lifting a rosette in spring, preferably with some root attached, and replanting in a shady, moist compost until thoroughly re-established. It is one of the many campanulas which is completely deciduous, and disappears in winter. Many have thought it dead and gone, and, digging its position during the dormant season, have made sure it is dead and gone!

C. *pulla* received an AM when shown in 1976.

C. X PULLOIDES

15cm • Dark blue • July

This is a garden hybrid - the two parents grow in nature some 300 km apart. As is so often *the case, C. carpatica* subsp. *turbinata* is one, and the last entry, *C. pulla*, the other. We would expect the latter to be the seed parent, as our subject resembles it the more closely of the two. There is the root-running habit and the deep flower colour of *C. pulla*. The basal rosettes are sparsely furnished, and the leaves larger than the latter; the stems bear few leaves, which are longer, and the stem height is greater – some 15-18cm. The

Left: *Campanula pulla*

flowers are of the same deep violet-blue colour, but more pendent, larger, and somewhat 'blowsy' in their shape, as if composed of slightly crinkled paper. The flowering is a couple of weeks later than *C. pulla*.

This is not a robust plant; it needs an open gritty soil, and it should be renewed constantly. If happy, a mat of it, preferably on a limestone scree, is an attractive feature of a raised bed.

C. PUNCTATA Lam.

30cm x 45cm • Pink/white • Summer

Whilst in some gardens this species can become a weed, in others it tends to die out without apparent cause. And one could be pardoned for wondering why it was formerly known as *C. nobilis*. However, when successful it does bear beautiful long bells with crimson specks and flecks within. The flowers are waxy cream outside; within, the crimson internal spots show through a little, sometimes to give a rather muddy effect. On a flourishing plant the flowers are freely and regularly hung like the decorations on a sparse Christmas tree.

Soft fleshy pointed heart-shaped leaves on long stalks arise from the rootstock in spring. The stems, 30cm or more in a vigorous form, bear similar but more or less stalkless leaves, and terminate with the pendent flowers abut 5cm long. The calyx lobes are triangular and lie flat to the corolla. The appendages are oval, reflexed and about half the length of the rest of the calyx.

The inside of the flower is really most

attractive, and success with its planting depends on placing it at or above eye-level so that the inside of the bell, with the rich red markings, can be seen. It has a clear preference for a sandy soil or a peaty one, though pining in heavy clay; it seems indifferent to lime.

This campanula comes from Siberia, China and Japan.

C. p. f. albiflora or 'Alba'
A white form and somewhat variable, but on the whole smaller than the type; can be confused with the following in cultivation. Some clones are low growing enough to be dubbed 'Alba Nana'.

C. p. var. chinensis
China and Siberia. This form, as we have handled it from collectors, is less robust, the stems are lighter, and the flowers smaller and less richly marked.

C. p. var. hondoensis
The Japanese form, described as subspecies or var. *hondoensis*. It is in general considerably larger than the Siberian form, and the fact that it also lacks appendages may justify taxonomic separation. To the gardener it just makes for a larger, sometimes more ungainly version of C. *punctata*.

C. p. var. impunctata
A variety found described in Japanese floras. The flowers are creamy white throughout except for the slightest red patch on the tips of the petals. We have

found it to be dwarf, one of the most attractive variants of the species, and a good alpine grower's specimen.

C. p. var. microdonta
This plant is smaller and paler, and the whole plant less hairy.

C. p. var. rubriflora (as recognised in taxonomic literature, but also often 'Rubriflora'/'Rubra').
Here the veining on the outside of the corolla is also red, while the interior colouring is also more liberally scattered and deeper, so that overall the flower gives a much darker red impression. It is very floriferous, but again varies in size.

As may be inferred from all this, C. *punctata* is clearly very variable in form. Thus 'Pallida', 'Rosea' etc have been proffered as names; in the garden, any of these will hybridise with any other, giving a miscellany of intermediates *ad infinitum*.

C. *punctata* has also given rise to the better C. 'Burghaltii' and C. 'Van Houttei'. These are crosses, it is surmised, between C. *punctata* and C. *latifolia*. The former probably has C. *punctata* as the pollen parent, the latter as the seed parent. They are described separately.

Synonym: C. *nobilis* Lindley

C. PYRAMIDALIS L.
122-150cm x 70cm • Blue, White • July/Aug
Cultivation of the Chimney Bellflower reached its height in the 19th century, and it

Campanula punctata 'Rubriflora'

was much grown in Victorian and Edwardian times as a house-plant. Its huge size was its attraction, as it was brought into the hall or drawing room and stood in the empty chimney breast. This idea has rather overshadowed its use as a hardy plant for the back of the border, where it can reach monstrous proportions. It does not please everyone, however: Christopher Lloyd wrote: 'The reason they are unsuccessful in the garden is because the bees pollinate their flowers, and these then fade in a matter of three days instead of three weeks. All campanulas are similarly bee-inflicted and are well worth growing as pot plants for indoor use, whenever possible.' [21]

C. pyramidalis comes from northern Italy and the north-west of the Balkan peninsula. It is strictly perennial, but short-lived. The plant is glabrous, with usually one, but often several stems rising erect to about 122cm. The basal leaves are broadly ovate, toothed, on long stems which form a pyramid of numerous flowering spikes. The stem leaves are stalkless and oval to lance-shaped. The many flowers are small, 5cm wide, broadly lobed bells, blue or white in colour. The long flower stems hold the starry flowers erect, the styles thrusting forward beyond the petals. The calyx is smooth and about half as long as the petals.

C. pyramidalis is easy to grow. Seed sown in April and planted out will flower in its second year. In the border it needs a shady moist soil, and adequate staking as it may snap at the base in high winds. For the authors it self-sows modestly, and seems to have an affinity for cracks in paving, which is not unpleasant.

In 1892 a form called A. p. 'Compacta' received an AM, as did C. p. 'Alba' in 1896.

The following notes are from the Gardeners' Chronicle of 1845:

This plant, when properly treated will produce a flowering stem from eight to 16 feet [250-500cm] in height, regularly branching from the bottom upwards, and forming a pyramid which is of singular beauty when the blossoms are expanded.

Seed should be sown in March in pans, and then pricked out in rich light soil where they should remain until they begin to grow in the following spring. The strongest plants may be selected for potting; as the plants are not intended to flower until they are two years old, they should at first be put in pots just large enough to prevent the roots from being cramped, and to induce a slow but healthy growth. They should remain through the winter in a pot no larger than eight inches [20cm]. The treatment during the winter months is to plunge the pots in sand or ashes in a frame where they can be kept dry. On about 20th March... the season has arrived when the plants are to be shifted into pots in which they are to flower, and as they will have to be moved from place to place, the pots should not be larger than one man can conveniently carry when filled with soil.

Let the compost be 1/3 well rotted and dry hotbed dung, put through a coarse sieve, 1/3 turfy loam... and 1/3 sand; let these be well mixed together, and have ready a quantity of lime-rubbish, about the size of Filberts, or Walnuts; let the pot be well drained, then over the drainage place a layer of the lime rubbish, then the soil, on which place the plant with the ball entire, and as you proceed to fill the pot let handfuls of the lime-rubbish be scattered round it with the soil... great attention should be paid to free the soil of worms. The plants should now be placed in a cold frame, and the light kept close, admitting a little air when the sun shines, with an occasional watering overhead to produce vigorous growth. When the stem has grown four or six inches (10-13cm), the plant

Right: Campanula pyramidalis

*should be removed to the late vinery where fires
are seldom used. The shade and proper treatment
of the vines in a house of this description are
admirably adapted for the vigorous growth and
elongation of the flower-stem; when it has
attained its greatest height, the plant should be
gradually exposed to more light, which will give
strength to the stem and colour to the blossom,
and if circumstances have been favourable, it
will excite the admiration of everybody.* [22]

This Victorian artifice seems complex
enough, but is rewarding.

C. p. 'Aureo-variegata'

A form with yellow blotched leaves, offered
until recently by one nursery. This must be
propagated vegetatively. We found it 'miffy'.

C. RADDEANA Trautvetter
35cm x 25cm • Bright blue • July/Aug

Another Caucasian, bearing the name of
its first collector, G. Radde. Running roots
form mats of rosettes of dark green shiny
leaves which are triangular to heart-shaped,
toothed, and on long petioles. A fine stem,
often of a deep wine-coloured tinge, arises
from each rosette; this carries similar but
shorter-stalked leaves and a raceme of
large, drooping deep violet-purple bells.
The petals are lobed to one-third of their
length (about 2cm). The calyx has
triangular appendages, and the three-part
style is the same length as the corolla. The
pollen is of a characteristic orange colour.

A thoroughly colourful and attractive
small plant which won an AM in 1908,

when shown by Reuthe. It merits
cultivation today. It is at its best in a well-
drained, sunny position, in a soil which is
not so rich as to promote leaf-growth at the
expense of flower; if the front of a small
border can provide this, it will thrive. It is
seen and appreciated better when nearer to
eye-level. It is a strong lime-lover, related to
C. kemulariae, but without the least
tendency to hide its bells amongst the
foliage as this latter.

Seed is sometimes set, and it will self-
sow, but such propagation is not to be
counted on; pieces of the rooting runners
taken in spring with the beginnings of a
rosette attached will not fail to establish
quickly. Indeed, it tends to be a vigorous
runner, and may need watching on this
account.

Synonym: *C. brotheri* Somm. & Levier

C. RAINERI Perpenti AGM
8cm • Blue • July

The most difficult aspect of this little
treasure is finding the real thing! It is
endemic to a very restricted area of the
Bergamo region of the southeastern Alps,
where it runs slowly in crevices in the
limestone rock and in scree to throw up
tufts of mid-green leaves, slightly but very
regularly toothed in a quite characteristic
manner, reminding one perhaps – in this
character only – of a *Dryas* leaf. Stems
some 8cm in height are thrown up, and
these are terminated by an unexpectedly
large open saucer of a blue flower.

Campanula raddeana

In cultivation, the ubiquitous *C. carpatica* crosses all too easily with this little plant, so that, unless open pollination can in some way be prevented, guarantees go with the wind as easily as the bees carry the pollen. The result of this hybridisation is what has been called *C. x pseudoraineri*, described above.

C. raineri is completely deciduous and quite hardy; it rejoices in the good drainage of a limestone scree. It creeps only slowly and is best in a sunny but slightly sheltered place where it will spring up each year. Watering should be generous during growth and flowering, and the area should not be allowed to become too dry at any time. On the other hand, winter wet allowed to hang around will surely kill – as with all true alpines, drainage and root-oxygenation are all important. *C. raineri* is not all that happy in a pot, or not for long without being moved on; this may be done in spring when growth restarts, with rooted underground runners being taken off for propagation.

First find your plant; although *C. raineri* is perhaps a connoisseur's plant, it is not too difficult to cultivate, but unless the leaf is quite emphatically longer than its width, and only slightly and regularly toothed, one must be suspicious of an intrusion of *C. carpatica*. Seed from a dependable source is probably the best guarantee, unless a reliable pedigree is offered with the plant.

C. RAPUNCULOIDES L.

100cm x 45cm • Blue • June/Sept

'The most insatiable and irrepressible of beautiful weeds. If once its tall and arching spires of violet bells prevail on you to admit it to your garden, neither you nor its choice inmates will ever know peace again.' (23) Thus Farrer sums up and dismisses *C. rapunculoides*. Well, 'ever' is a long time.

This plant owes its success to a mass of thick white dahlia-like roots which spread at an alarming rate in light soils, and penetrate deeply. In addition, it seeds abundantly, and the light seeds are blown a great distance. In 1901 the *Gardeners' Chronicle* advised that 'no thistle or dock... is worse, and that no nurseryman should be allowed to sell it. One tradesman who was remonstrated with replied that he had a demand for it – 'to kill grass'. (24) A recent garden visitor confirmed this ability to kill grass, but we cannot recommend it... *C. rapunculoides* roots do in effect quite fill a bed, strangling all competition; though the prospect of watching combat between *C. rapunculoides* and twitch is reminiscent of the sadism of the ancient amphitheatre. Despite such warning, it is too often a fact that the plant is acquired by accident, usually wrongly named. Adenophoras are not infrequently found to be this when well established and already a well-established menace. Then it has to be eradicated. One of us has more than once received it in this way, but it was of a clone that appears to be less pernicious than Farrer's. It took only one season to eliminate it from a bed of 3½ x 1m (11½ x 3ft). This was done with a fork and hoe

Campanula rapunculoides 'Alba'

without resorting to herbicides, but at the cost of the bed looking somewhat bare during that season! For those who use it, glyphosate would have been quicker.

Having given the warning and the remedy, it has to be admitted that the plant is beautiful.

The basal leaves are long-pointed, heart-shaped on long stalks, but wither when the stems elongate. The stem-leaves are stalkless and broadly lance-shaped. All leaves have prominent veins on the underside, and are lightly toothed. The flowers 2-2½cm long, are borne in a raceme, horizontal or drooping on a short stalk. Calyx lobes are lance-shaped, strongly reflexed at flowering but have no appendages. The style is in three parts and the same length as the corolla, the lobes of which are divided to one-third, pointed and slightly reflexed.

C. rapunculoides occurs naturally in most of Europe, Iran, Caucasus, Central Asia and Siberia. It is found naturalised in Britain, Scandinavia and America, often on waste ground. Occurring over such a range, it is somewhat variable in size, leaf and flower shape and invasiveness.

In Russia it has been considered as a cure for hydrophobia. We offer no details.

C. r. 'Alba'

Not frequently seen; we cultivate this in Cambridgeshire, where it is shorter (45-60cm), much less vigorous than the type, and quite manageable. The flowers, which last longer than the type, are a pure virgin white, and while seed is freely set, we have not known it to germinate; a fail-safe plant which must therefore be propagated by division in spring.

Synonyms: *C. cordifolia* Koch.; *C. rhomboidea* Falk.; *C. rhomboidalis* Gorter; *C. trachelioides* Reichenb.; *C. setosa* Fisch.

A number of subspecific names have been applied, some of them referable to the above. It may be added that many unrepeatable vernacular names have also been used by gardeners.

C. RAPUNCULUS L.

60-90cm x 30cm • White to lilac • April

The rampion (not to be confused with *Phyteuma* also commonly called rampion) was once grown as an autumn and winter vegetable, and reportedly still is in the former Yugoslavia. The name is a diminutive of the Latin *rapum* – turnip.

A usually hairless biennial, with a thickened root. The basal leaves are oval, widest at the middle, pointed, 4cm long, on long winged petioles. The flowers are small and narrowly bell-shaped, 2-2½cm long, divided by one-third into pointed lobes, and hairless. They are whitish to pale blue, on short thin pedicels and are held in long spikes. The calyx teeth are long (nearly as long as the petals) and very narrow, rather like bristles; there are no appendages. The style is almost as long as the corolla, and it divides into three stigmas.

This very variable plant is widespread over most of Europe (except the extreme north), South and Central Russia,

Caucasus, Crimea, Turkey, Syria, Iran and North Africa.

C. *rapunculus* features in the fairy tale by the Brothers Grimm, *Rapunzel*, where a pregnant peasant girl yearned for vegetables that she could see in the garden next to her. A high wall surrounded the garden, which belonged to a witch. The young woman became obsessed with desire for the fine salad vegetables, and so she began to pine

Campanula rapunculus root

away. Her husband climbed the wall to steal them, and the first time the witch apparently did not see him. However, the next time she was waiting for him. She caught him and made him promise to bring her his child when it was born, in return for letting him have the salads. The young wife gave birth to a fine girl, who was named Rapunzel after the vernacular name still popular for the plant.

In 1918 *The Garden* magazine reported that seed was widely available. [25] It advised sowing thinly in April or May in a rich shady soil. The plants mature in October when the root is about 1cm thick, and 12cm long, like a small carrot, but white. Sown as a row in the vegetable garden by one of us, germination was good. The plants flowered early and freely, but by summer they had gone to seed and looked untidy. Many of the roots forked, but the best had a pungent nutty flavour. Also with us it self-sows each year in a paved garden, and we would miss this modest little plant if it ever failed us. The roots have been popular cooked or raw since Middle Ages, but the seed is now only likely to be found from the Societies, or from specialists.

Several subspecies and varieties have been described for this variable plant, including subsp. *lambertiana* Boiss. and var. *spiciformis* Boiss. Neither is in cultivation.

C. 'R. B. LODER'
8cm x 15cm • Pale blue • July

This is a double *C. cochlearifolia* very like 'Elizabeth Oliver' already mentioned, but occurred back in the 1920s; it has a flower more closely bunched and much paler in colour – an ice blue. Apart from this there is little difference in foliage or habit; though it tends to be slightly taller; but this depends on cultivation conditions, and especially exposure to sun.

C. RHOMBOIDALIS L.
To 45cm x 20cm • Blue • July/Sept

This is a neglected plant. It has fallen into a niche where, too big for the small modern rock-garden, too small for the border, and unhappy for long in a pot, it remains unheralded and so unknown. Unknown that is, except by those 'who have seen the alpine fields one undulating sea of sapphire waves beneath its sheaves of deep noble blue harebells gathered loosely toward the top of those stalwart stems, clothed in rhomboidal toothy foliage all the way up'. So said Farrer, whose apt description could hardly be bettered, and who continues: 'In cultivation this beautiful thing is no less stalwart and splendid in any border, but its two feet or 18 inches (40-60cm) fit it chiefly for bolder sweeps in the rock-garden, among such old friends and neighbours as *Anemone alpina* (*Pulsatilla alpina*).' [26] It is native to the central and southwestern Alps, but is widely naturalised elsewhere. Above all it is too often confused with *C. rotundifolia*, though they are really quite different.

It is firmly perennial, growing from a turnip-like root with branching rhizomes, which spread only slowly. The clump of basal leaves is often persistent in winter, but disappears at flowering; they are stalked, while the stem-leaves are stalkless. The leaves being diamond-shaped, the stems appear better clothed than those of C. rotundifolia: and also much stouter. Flowers are in a raceme, not numerous, and about 2cm long, divided to one-quarter their length, and of a deep purple-blue. Calyx lobes are linear, smooth, much reflexed and without appendages; the three-part style is the same length as the corolla.

By itself it only spreads slowly, but pieces of rhizome with roots may be lifted in spring for an increase in plants. Seed is set but, like that of many a beautiful campanula, is not offered except by specialists. It loves the sun and, happy, will flower for a long period. In Cambridgeshire in a mild autumn it has flowered in exposed places on the rock garden into December.

There were, in Farrer's day, many named cultivars, but these remain untraceable today.

C. ROTUNDIFOLIA L.

40cm • Blue • Summer

C. rotundifolia is, to the gardener, an all-embracing term. It occurs in nature throughout the northern hemisphere north of the tropics, and tends to receive a local name wherever it is described. Flora Europaea splits it into some 20-odd, to

which, no doubt the observant gardener would probably add even more. Some names derive from the area in which it occurs, and whilst we agree with the botanists that differences are real, they are on such a scale that the gardener may wisely ignore them. No doubt if they were more dramatic plants, or something of a challenge to grow, there would be more reason, or excuse, for going into the finer details of shape and size leaf, erect or pendent bells, and whether these are followed by pendent or erect capsules; permutations the scrutiny of which may well dishearten the gardener while his weeds keep growing... There is many a different plant which has no special claim to fame apart from the fact that it provides a challenge to the specialist alpine grower; C. rotundifolia is not found among their number, but one outstanding plant is C. linifolia 'Covadonga' (though the linifolia is now obsolete). Collected in the Covadonga National Park in northern Spain, and introduced by Clarence Elliott and Dr Roger Bevan, it is a somewhat sprawling little plant with wiry stems and pointed oval basal leaves and longer, finer stem leaves with three to four teeth to each margin, all on long petioles, and terminated by a largish bell of a deep violet blue. Height of the true plant is some 8cm when grown in stony conditions.

The native British harebell, the Scottish Bluebell – a name which is repeated in most European languages – remains one of our best wildflowers:

Campanula rotundifolia in the Massif Central of France

With buds, and bells, and stars without a name,
With all the gardener Fancy e'er could feign,
Who breeding flowers, will never breed the same.
Keats

Rotundifolia translates as 'round-leaved'. Many an innocent observer has failed to find the round leaves, which, in fact, are usually withered away at the time of flowering, the remaining visible ones being only variable in how long and narrow they can be. The plant can be grown in any soil (or lack of it), where it will form a large round clump before setting out to spread far and wide, also seeding quite generously;

but no gardener who can operate a hoe need feel menaced. Apart from the varying shades of blue – most frequently pale – there are records of doubles, and also white variants; but in spite of the wide distribution of this aggregate, these are not often encountered in the wild. There are, however, reliable reports in the past of the following:

C. r. var. alaskana

This has been described as bearing a larger flower on a shorter stem, as has var. *groenlandica* but from the seed available as such we have found little variation from the type.

C. r. 'Alba'

An albino form, which comes largely true from seed. We grow this robust little plant,

Campanula 'Covadonga'

Campanula rotundifolia 'Alba'

which forms a dense tuft; it is freely available.

C. r. 'Olympica' comes from the Olympics in the state of Washington, USA, where it is said to be very variable, but at its best is a robust 22cm tall, wide-belled campanula with dark green, rather jagged leaves. It was introduced to British commerce by Ingwersen.

C. r. 'Soldanelloides'
With the bell slit into numerous narrow segments, like the corolla of a Soldanella, it

was stated to be a 'freak' which the writer (in the 'Garden') had lost. Can it be refound?

As *C. rotundiflolia* is so very widely distributed, it is hardly surprising that it is so variable; the surprise is that it is not in fact more so. The botanists distinguish many forms, but we tend to finish up where we started this account of the species – all-embracing. William Sutherland, manager of the herb department at Kew, writing in the *Handbook of Hardy Herbs and Alpine Flowers* in 1871 has the last word: 'Though not very far-fetched, this plant so wonderfully increases in beauty under care and culture that I cannot pass it over in this list without strongly recommending it to those who may not have given it a trial.' [27]

It is eminently suited to the rock-garden, and the smaller members of what we have treated as the *rotundifolia* group may be grown very effectively in raised beds, and even more so in sinks and troughs; in any case, it does best in a poor gritty soil, in crevices or in tufa, as in nature. For such use, we have had good experience of *C. carnica* from the southern Alps; *C. justiniana* from the former Yugoslavia; *C. recta* from the Pyrenees, *C. scheuchzeri*, which is widely distributed from Pyrenees and Alps to Carpathians, usually with larger flowers; *the neat C. baumgartenii* from the Vosges which keeps its round basal leaves until flowering. These and others like them freely cross in the garden, losing their individual characteristics.

C. SARMATICA Ker-Gawl.

50cm x 40cm • Grey-blue • May/July

This perennial comes from rocky and stony slopes at alpine and sub-alpine levels in the Caucasus.

A large clump of coarse, wrinkled and crumpled, hairy grey-green leaves, triangular and pointed in shape with a heart-shaped base, and petioles that are longer than the leaf blades gives rise to several stout unbranched hairy stems, and these bear similarly shaped, but smaller, stemless leaves. The pale blue or blue-grey flowers are borne in one-sided conical racemes. They are bell-shaped with flaring lobes, bearded within, each of which shows an even more hairy nerve-line. The calyx is of bristly lobes hugging the corolla tube and half its length. It has short triangular appendages which are reflexed in a continuation of the line of the main calyx lobes. The three-part style equals the length of the corolla.

The effect is of a rugged plant, soundly hardy and perennial; perhaps a little coarse, but quietly attractive. It is well-placed in the forward part of the border or in the rock-garden, and it has been suggested that it looks particularly well against a background of paler green conifers. It has something of the habit of a smaller *C. alliariifolia* to which it is, of course, closely related botanically. It can take a little more sun than some campanulas, and is found also to be unattractive to slugs, possibly because of the hairs.

C. sarmatica cannot be propagated by division, growing as it does from a single

Campanula sarmatica

rootstock; seed is, however, plentifully set, from which fresh plants may be easily raised. It was introduced in 1805, and figured in the *Botanical Magazine*, t. 2019.

C. *sarmatica* should not be confused with *C. sarmentosa*, a synonym of *C. rigidipila* from Ethiopia and the highlands of Kenya (and, incidentally, the most southerly occurring campanula). Sarmatia is an old name for the southern part of European Russia.

Synonyms: *C. albiflora* C. Koch (white form); *C. betonicifolia*.

C. SAXATILIS L.   AGM
15cm x 20cm • Blue • June/July

This is a Cretan endemic, growing in rock crevices in the mountains. A thick carrot-like root throws a tuft of sage-green spathulate leaves on a simple petiole, from among which numerous more or less prostrate flowering stems with small sessile leaves give rise to a raceme of upright trumpet-shaped flowers of light blue, showing often a darker blue bar down their centres. They have slightly reflexed pointed lobes, an enclosed style and five stigmas. The smooth calyx has short, blunt appendages.

This is an alpine gardener's plant which takes well to a pot in the alpine house, and is perennial and hardy, but in our experience not long-lived.

C. SAXIFRAGA

This has been referred to under *C. aucheri*. We are well aware that there are taxonomic differences between the species of this aggregate, but have only a restricted faith in the names in commerce, and in cultivation.

C. SIBIRICA L.
50cm x 30cm • Pale blue • July/Aug

This plant occurs over a much wider range than the name suggests - all over Eastern Europe, through to the Crimea, and over most of Russia. Growing as it does under such differing conditions, it is extremely variable.

It is a biennial or monocarpic species, taking two or even three years in cultivation to flower. It is a hairy plant throughout. A single or several stems, according to form, arise from a basal rosette of lance-shaped or oblong to lance-shaped leaves with winged petioles. The stem leaves are lance-shaped and stalkless. The stems are sometimes branched above and bear flowers terminally and on short pedicales in the leaf-axils. These flowers may be numerous, or borne singly, and are of a bluish-lilac colour, sometimes nearly white, the corolla forms a more or less funnel-shaped bell 15-20 mm long, with flaring lobes, sometimes hairy within. The calyx lobes are pointed and bristly, the appendages reflexed. It is variable, like many characteristics of the plant, in size and shape. The three-part style is about the same length as the corolla.

Campanula saxifraga

C. *sibirica* can be grown from seed, and it is not an unattractive plant when grown en masse. It has recently been offered early in the season as a house plant.

C. SPECIOSA Pourr.

46cm x 30cm • Blue, White • July

This is a plant which has been neglected of recent years, but which could well fill a useful and colourful place in the narrower borders of today's smaller gardens. It was introduced in 1820, much grown for years, and received an Award of Merit in 1928; yet it remains relatively unknown today. Almost anyone could be forgiven for thinking it a dwarf compact Canterbury Bell.

A large, flat rosette of narrowly lance-shaped leaves throws up a stout and bristly leafy stem, less branched than the Canterbury Bell; the stem leaves are narrower, and stalkless. The relatively large, well-proportioned bell-shaped

Campanula sibirica

flowers, 1½cm long, are borne on individual
pedicels; these are very long at the base,
and gradually decrease in length up the
stem, so that the effect is of a pyramidal
spike of flowers. The flowers are blue or
white. We have not heard of the pink
shades seen in the Canterbury Bell, but this
shade could well appear, as in other
species, if *C. speciosa* were grown more.
The calyx lobes are short, narrow with
reflexed stubby appendages. The style is in
three parts (which distinguishes it from the
five of *C. medium*) and is about the same
length as the corolla.

This plant has been described as
perennial *(Flora Europaea)* and monocarpic
(RHS Dictionary) with which Crook
agrees. With us it has never been other than
the latter, although it may take several
seasons to flower. It prefers a gritty soil,
and it must have a warm sunny spot to give
of its best, as it does in the rocky limestone
soils of the Cévennes, Corbières and
Eastern Pyrenees from which it comes, and
where summer holidaymakers may well
have spotted it.

If *C. speciosa* is to be used in the
border, it is best raised in pots with some
winter protection to prevent rotting at the
crown, though it needs no heat. It can then
be planted out in spring, when it will make
a magnificent display. Grown in a gritty
stony scree, top-dressed around the
vulnerable collar, winter wet will probably
not harm it. It is worth the trouble.

Synonyms: *C. allionii* Lapeyr.; *C. barbata*
Lapeyr.

C. affinis Roem. & Schultes

This is a closely related and easily confused
plant; it comes from a similar area, though
more common to the south of the range of
C. speciosa. Flora Europaea describes it as
coming from the mountains of eastern
Spain, whilst its subspecies *bolosii* (Vayr.)
Fedorov, also referred to in the past as *C.
bolosii* Vayr., has its home on Montserrat.
These two tend to have more open, flatter
corollas.

There is a good modern description and
illustration of *C. affinis* in the *Botanical
Magazine* at t. 9568.

C. 'STANSFIELDII' Auct.
12cm • Violet-blue • July

The parentage of this old hybrid is
obscure, but it is thought to be a cross
between *C. tommasiniana* and, perhaps, *C.
carpatica*. It forms mats of pale green,
hairy, somewhat diamond-shaped leaves
and throws up stems of 10 or 12cm in
height scattered on the spreading mat.
These stems are each topped by shallow
but wide violet bells, pendent and with
corolla lobes divided to about one-third
their depth and well reflexed. As well as
being 'a gift of heaven... a treasure of the
highest claims'[2] (Farrer extravaganza!) this
little plant has been the parent of other
useful hybrids, including *C.* 'Norman
Grove'. In itself, it is a beautiful, long-lived
cushion plant.

Farrer suggests that it may in fact be a
natural hybrid, and he puts forward the
names of *C. c. tommasiniana* or

waldsteiniana with *C. pulla* as the possible parents, occurring as they do at one point on common ground on Monte Maggiore in northern Italy. Evidence in favour of this was his claim that batches of plants of these species (sent from there in days when such collections from nature were not frowned upon) contained some of this apparent cross. This must remain something of a mystery, albeit an interesting one, as, although the literature contains many mentions of our *C. x stansfieldii*, little is said which helps to solve the problem. Because we are inclined to accept the theory, however, we retain the form of its name given here.

C. TAKESIMANA Naikai
70cm x 40cm • Red, Pink, White • July/Sept

This is a plant which, described in a *Flora of Korea* as long ago as 1922, was more recently collected and introduced from the island of Ullung-Do, in the Sea of Japan off Korea. Careful publicity moved it on to the NCCPG 'Pink List' of plants rare in cultivation, but such is its habit that it has rapidly romped off this list.

Campanula 'Stansfieldii'

A strong, creeping rootstock throws up at intervals rosettes of flourishing fleshy heart-shaped leaves, often with a reddish tinge, borne on a petiole usually much longer than the blade itself. This petiole is lightly winged, and also toothed at intervals. The whole is a bright glossy green, and the leaf-surfaces are markedly veined. Strong upright or angled stems, frequently tinged maroon, bear a few more or less sessile, but similarly shaped leaves, and, in the leaf-axils and at the tips, yellowish buds develop into long tubular bells of a pale greyish-pink with maroon inner markings reminiscent of C. punctata, to which it is no doubt closely related. Calyx-lobes are long, pointed, with appendages.

This is a handsome plant preferring a moist open sandy or peaty soil; in this it is inclined to be rampant, and will consequently require some supervision. In our clay we find it well-behaved (or even inclined to die out, as does C. punctata) and, although it sets seed, it scatters this very little. In any case, so far as propagation is concerned, it is hardly needful to gather seed, as pieces of the running root, preferably with a node and rosette, are very easily established.

In cultivation the species varies widely in colouring, from deep maroon to a palid pink; a sowing of seeds demonstrates this strikingly. Campanula 'Elizabeth' is a selection of this species found in the nursery of Elizabeth Strangman in Kent. This has particularly rich maroon flowers with still deeper maroon markings both inside and out, and is a fine plant.

C. THYRSOIDES L.

30-70cm x 30cm • Yellow • July/Aug

This is one of the few campanulas which is never blue. Its other immediate distinction is its habit – a thyrse, being a closely branched flowering stem with many short-stalked flowers. This thyrse is formed of a much longer cluster of flowers than seen in C. glomerata. The basal rosette is of wavy oblong to lance-shaped leaves. The stem rising from its centre is stout, erect and unbranched, with closely packed, very bristly lance-shaped leaves; sometimes there is more than one stem from the rosette, but usually one is dominant. These stem-leaves become shorter higher on the stem, to the point of being but bracts in the axils of which arise the flowers; all so close as to form a compact steeple.

Individual flowers are with only slightly reflexed petal lobes. The calyx teeth are very narrow and there are no appendages. There are three stigmas, and an ovary in three sections.

The colour is said to be yellowish-white, or pale straw, but there is a subspecies carniolica, where the flowers are not so compacted together that is, the internodes are longer, the bracts are longer, and indeed the whole inflorescence and stem are longer – in cultivation up to 1m (three feet). The claims of the species to our attention may be summed up in the concise assessment of an American lady visitor 'Well, it sure is interesting!'

Campanula takesimana 'Elizabeth'

C. thyrsoides is seen at its best planted in close groups in the border, where it is utterly hardy, and where it sets seed abundantly. As it is biennial in habit, seed is the only way to propagate, and this is easy.

Mountain walkers will have seen *C. thyrsoides* in the high meadows from the Jura through the Alps and into the Balkan mountains.

The plant is portrayed in the *Botanical Magazine* at t. 1290, named *thyrsoidea*.

C. t. ssp. *carniolica* (Suend.) Podl.

Is found particularly, as the name suggests, in the Carniolic Alps bordering Austria, Italy and the former Yugoslavia. It has been suggested in the past that this subspecies is a richer yellow shade, but the flora do not substantiate this, and no doubt there is variability in this factor across the species. It is a taller plant.

C. TOMMASINIANA Koch

10cm x 15cm • Lavender • Aug

This attractive little species hails from northwest Slovenia, where it grows in rocky mountain woodland. A thick perennial root throws up numerous branching wiry stems bearing lance-shaped and lightly toothed leaves and a mass of hanging, somewhat tubular bells of pale blue. It can be one of the later flowerers, but it is not difficult in cultivation. It seems to thrive in any well-drained position, in sun or shade; it will be happy in a pot, a sink or open scree. It is a lime-lover. Runners are given off very sparingly from the main root, and these

may be used for propagation, when taken off in spring, generally with some fine root-hairs already formed, but it is more easily grown from seed. A characteristic feature of this little plant is the almost horny tip to the leaf.

C. TRACHELIUM L.

45-90cm x 30cm • Blue-purple, White • July/August

Bats-in-the-Belfrey is a native, but not common, campanula in the wild in Britain. It is scattered in woods and hedgerows through the southern UK and Europe. (It is replaced in northern Britain by *C. latifolia*.) 'Nettled-leaved' is more descriptive than the 'Bats' term Farrer used.

The rootstock is woody, and the rough, acutely angled stems often emerge from a single base, a limiting factor when it comes to division of the plant for vegetative propagation. The leaves are bristly, and nettle-shaped, but happily they lack the sting. The lower leaves sit on long petioles; those higher on the stem are shorter, and the leaves smaller. The flowers are tubular, bell-shaped and slightly hairy, with the lobes dividing to about one-third. The calyx lobes are linear to lance-shaped, and there are no appendages. The seed capsule is round, nodding, and opens at the base. The flowers are rather like those of *C. latifolia* but not quite so long.

This may be thought too leafy and coarse a plant for the formal garden, but it looks well naturalised in grass or light woodland, and is not invasive at the root,

Campanula trachelium 'Alba Plena'

though it does produce a lot of seedlings. Propagation by seed is easy and can result in light blue or white. The white form is attractive as its flowers show up rather better against the leaves. An alkaline clay soil which is slightly moist seems to suit all forms best, but it is not essential.

C. t. 'Alba Flore Plena'
60cm x 30cm • White • June

A delicious cottage garden plant, which shows off its semi-double white cup-shaped, fringed flowers to perfection against the light green leaves. It is quite tall and strong, and can usually be relied upon to flower very freely. Division is the only method of propagation, and it takes some courage to lift the plant and slice through the woody stem with a knife; this should be done in spring as new growth commences, or in July after cutting the stems back to their base and teasing the new shoots apart carefully; this last has been found to be reliable, and is even more so if the stems are cut back before flowering (at cost of no flowers for that season; but it's worth it).

There seems to be more than one form of this in circulation. In the best the bell is as wide as it is deep, and the petals reflex strongly.

C. t. 'Bernice'
40-60cm x 30cm • Lilac-blue • June

This double C. trachelium has been known since the late 16th century. The flowers are double, deep amethyst-coloured. The delightfully fringed cup-shaped bell gives the impression of a flounced crinoline. It flowers profusely for a long time, with the flowers held well above the leaves. It is quite tough and hardy, and can be propagated by division, with care, as it is slow to increase. It will sometimes come true from seed. 'Bernice' was re-introduced by Alan Bloom, who received it with the name C. lariaefolia which seems invalid. Its only faults are a slightly stiff habit, and an attraction for blackfly.

A bicoloured double form has been illustrated in old accounts, but we have never seen it, nor heard of its present existence.

Synonyms: C. urticifolia/C. urticaefolia Schm.
(It should be noted that these names has also been applied by different writers to C. bononiensis, C. latifolia and C. rapunculoides, all of which, of course, have nettle-like leaves.)

C. TROEGERAE Damboldt
25cm x 30cm • White • July

This, a recently described relative of C. betulifolia from Turkey, has found favour with the alpine grower. The leaves are thicker and fleshier than those of C. betulifolia, slightly greyer, and often with stronger teeth. The main difference is in the flowers, which are here rotated, with triangular and pointed lobes divided to two-thirds, usually white, but sometimes, like its relative, with pinkish tinges, mainly in the bud. There are small triangular calyx appendages. This is an excellent plant in a

Campanula trachelium 'Bernice'

pot for the alpine house, but is very hardy, and has prospered for many years with us on a rock garden, where it is grown on the north side of a shading rock. *C. choruhensis* is similar, but differs in having the lobes of the corolla divided only to one-third, making it superficially closer to *C. betulifolia*, and having no appendages.

This may be acquired as seed or as a young plant; it is not easy to divide at any time, but sets seed well, and is best propagated by sowing this over winter. It will usually flower modestly in its first season.

C. 'TYMONSII'
12cm • China blue • Aug

This is a neat little hybrid between improbable parents, and quite different from the product of another get-together, C. 'John Innes'. The offenders are C.

Campanula troegerae

carpatica, of well-proven promiscuity, and *C. pyramidalis*. Whatever the skeletons in the cupboard, the result is a success on the rock-garden, for the evidence of *C. pyramidalis* is scant to the view. A slowly, but not menacingly spreading, mat of toothed oval and bluntly pointed leaves of glossy green on stems which extend to some 10-12cm and are thickly topped by open, shallow and chubby bells of china blue; one of the truest blues of the campanulas. It is in our experience the latest of all to flower, and thus is all the more welcome in the garden.

This plant is beloved of the slug and the snail, and is best grown where these can be more easily controlled, such as in sinks and troughs; a limestone scree also provides ideal conditions for growth, and from this the runners may be gently pulled in spring for propagation.

It would appear from older accounts that two other campanulas of the same or similar parentage were known – these are *C.* 'Fergusonii' and *C.* 'Hendersonii', but these seem now to be lost. Inadequate descriptions make the location of such plants almost impossible.

C. 'VAN HOUTTEI' Hort.

40cm x25cm • Violet-blue • June/July

This is an old hybrid, often mentioned in books on campanula, and 'the other half' of *C.* 'Burghaltii' – that is the reverse cross between *C. latifolia* and *C. punctata*, the former here being the seed parent, and the colour following the flowers of this parent,

which are deeper than those of *C.* 'Burghaltii', and being variously described as indigo-blue or lavender-blue. It is now uncommon in cultivation, and we are not quite certain that the few plants which are grown are actually the real thing.

The leaves are long, oval to lance-shaped, with deeply notched margins. They are up to 10cm long and 3-4cm wide, hairy, with strong veins. The flowers are the same colour in bud and flower, are very large, up to 6cm long, and hang in a drooping raceme. They have narrow pointed calyx lobes, which are about 2cm long.

The origin of the plant is rather confused. It dates back to at least 1878, when it was said to have originated from Thibaut and Keteleer of Sceaux; others credit it to a Dr Rodigas, and to Messrs Van Houtte of Belgium. At least we know it was named after the respected Louis Van Houtte, one-time curator of the Royal Botanic Garden in Ghent, who later opened a nursery in France. The plant we have reference to is a mid-campanula blue.

Robin Lane Fox described the plant: 'My pleasure comes from an inky mauve variety called Van Houttei. This is quite unjustly ignored. It is a bolder colour and flowers profusely. You can mass it in the front of a border where its heavy crop of tubular flowers draws the eye. I consider it a very fine border plant indeed which splits easily into tens or 20s after a year'.[28] Like both its parents, it is at its best in a moist soil in partial shade. Margery Fish spoke of the plant dying out with her, but we have found that it will grow vigorously in a light

Campanula 'Tymonsii'

acid soil with plenty of moisture – in other words, that it is not easy, and wants the best of everything. Grown well, the plant has larger flowers and a more elegant habit than C. 'Kent Belle', which it closely resembles. It is well to keep in mind that, as with others of the older cultivars, there is material in circulation which is not quite true to name. With C. 'Van Houttei', some variants may indeed be the same cross, but not of the same clone as the original. This said, it would appear that the genuine thing is still with us.

C. VERSICOLOR Andrews

40cm x 20cm • Violet-Pale blue bicoloured • July/Aug

Unlike the leopard, campanulas can change their spots. C. versicolor is reported enthusiastically by some, and much less so by others. E. K. Balls was an enthusiast: 'The stems are thickly clothed with wide open stars. One and a half inches (4cm) across. They are a fine purplish blue with a white ring and a reddish flush in the centre. Some of these aged plants on high cliffs produce as many as 20 of these beautifully curved wands of bloom.' [29] It was discovered by John Sibthorp in the late 18th century, but was not in general cultivation until the 1930s. It received an AM in 1932.

The root is fleshy at first, later becoming woody and large as a fist, often wedged tightly between rocks in the wild. The basal leaves are smooth, oval to heart-shaped, notched and on long petioles. The stem leaves are on short petioles, and are narrower. Several leafy stems end in spikes of flowers. In the best plants these are clearly bicoloured, but some seedlings have less distinct colouring. They are wide saucer-shaped and with spreading lobes, the style projecting beyond them. Calyx lobes are narrow and reflexed. C. versicolor has a smell of cloves – one of the few campanulas with perfume.

The plant sets abundant seed, shed from valves at the base of the erect capsule, and seed is the best means of propagation. The species is very variable in the wild, and plants from seed need to be watched for the best forms.

C. versicolor is a cliff and mountain plant from Greece, Albania, the Balkans and southeast Italy. E. K. Balls wrote of it at 2,500m (8,000ft) in the Pindus range in Greece [29]. We have found it on sea cliffs in the Mani in Southern Greece.

C. x pyraversi

C. versicolor is more perennial than C. pyramidalis, which it resembles in form and habit, though being a smaller, more delicate plant. They cross to give what has been called C.x pyraversi, which is neither one thing nor the other and is singularly lacking in the way of virtues. We suspect that some plants offered as C. versicolor are, in fact, of this origin.

Campanula versicolor in the wild

C. WALDSTEINIANA Schultes

15cm X 20cm • Lavender blue • July

This is a neat little alpine plant from Dalmatia, where it grows in limestone rock-crevices in the mountains. In initial habit and appearance it closely resembles the tufted form of *C. tommasiniana*, but here the flowers are quite distinct, each stem showing a small cluster of upturned star-shaped bells, generally of a lighter blue than *C. tommasiniana*. The glabrous calyx has awl-shaped lobes, without appendages.

This is a long-lived plant which does particularly well in a rich calcareous gritty soil or a scree, and is reasonably happy in a pot if repotted annually.

C. 'WARLEY WHITE'

15cm x 25cm • White • Summer

There has been some confusion over the naming of this plant, which has been called *C. warleyensis, C.* 'Warley Alba' and *C. warleyensis alba.* There is little doubt that all refer to one and the same plant. This campanula originated in the garden of Miss Ellen Willmott in Warley, Essex, a seedling from *C.* 'Haylodgensis'. There is on record a somewhat indignant letter from Miss Willmott, who had shown the plant at the RHS Flower Show and received no Award, whilst a year or two later the same plant, shown by a nurseryman who also had a large trade exhibit at the show, obtained an AM. One of the complaints was of discrimination against the amateur; *plus ça change...*

C. 'Warley White' (which name we propose as the correct one, by reason of the Rules of Nomenclature, as well as the fact that it was awarded an AM under this name) is after the style of a lax *C. carpatica*, with stems of some 20cm which tend to tumble prostrately around the basal tuft. The sparse leaves are heart-shaped like those of this parent, but are of a characteristic yellowish-green shade. The flowers are semi- or fully-double, and are about 4cm across, open almost flat and held to the sun.

The plant has had a reputation for lack of hardiness, but this is far from the case, provided that it is so placed that winter dormancy is assured. This is best secured by a shaded or even northerly position, where the odd day of winter sun will not stimulate growth that will subsequently be scorched by frost. Any repetition of this rapidly exhausts a plant, and this has been recorded also for other small campanulas, such as *C.* 'G.F. Wilson' and *C.* 'Pseudoraineri'.

As mentioned, *C.* 'Warley White' obtained an AM when shown by Prichards of Highcliffe, in 1925. *C.* 'Warley' obtained a similar award in 1899, that time actually shown by Miss Willmott! This was blue, and also a seedling of *C.* 'Haylodgensis', but we have not been able to trace its survival.

C. VIDALII H C Watson

Correctly:– (and for over 100 years)

AZORINA VIDALII Feer
60cm x 30cm • Pink/white • Aug

The campanulate flowers reveal this as a member of the *Campanulaceae*, but a little different from most campanulas. Like others of the family from the Atlantic islands - Cap Verde Islands, Madeira and Azores, it is shrubby, with thickened, woody stems. We include it here for its intrinsic interest.

From a single woody stem there branch several side stems, scarred with the hardened bases of dead leaves, and reminiscent of an *Euphorbia*. The glossy linear leaves are notched, have indented veins, and form shining regular rosettes like a succulent (which, of course, they are). These elongate to form flowering spikes. The 3cm bells are on nodding, recurved stalks, are a subtle dusky pink, and are waisted at about their two-thirds their length. The waxy texture and waist give them the air of a plump Edwardian or Dickensian lady trying to be fashionable with her hour-glass figure. Inside the base of the flower the flat top of the ovary can be seen as a dramatic shining orange disc after pollination. Nearly white forms of the flowers are known, and even double forms with multiple petticoats which do not enhance the beauty of the hour-glass figure.

The stems do not branch again after flowering, and need to be cut out as they die off. Coming as it does from an Atlantic island, this plant is not frost-hardy, and must be overwintered in a conservatory or other bright spot where it can be kept from freezing. It is happy outside in summer, but prefers shelter from wind.

C. X WOCKEI 'Puck'
10cm • Blue • July

The parentage of this hybrid is probably *C. pulla* x *C. waldsteiniana*, although reliable accounts of its origin are hard to find. It is apparently closer to the former, and it is not impossible that it is a natural hybrid; for a brief discussion of this possibility, we refer to the entry on *C.* x *Stansfieldii*, to which it is related. It was introduced by Alan Bloom.

A winter resting-bud of tiny wedge-shaped leaves arising from underground runners enlarges in spring to form a rosette of oval leaves which throws up a stem some 10cm tall. This stem bears lance-shaped stalkless leaves, recalling those of the putative *C. waldsteiniana* parent, and terminates in a dangling deep blue bell.

The plant forms a slowly spreading diffuse mat, is reliably perennial, and is easily cultivated in an open soil with grit and some humus. It is also suitable for pot cultivation, but, like so many other campanulas, will be happier under these circumstances when repotted regularly each year.

C. ZOYSII Wulfen
8cm • Blue • July/Sept

Although this does not count among the easiest campanulas, it is so different that we have fallen into temptation, and so include it here. We cannot do better than quote Farrer: 'The last and strangest of the race – that minute exquisite rock-jewel which you may see filling the crevices and chinks of the Karawanken... rosettes of tiny

Campanula x *wockei* 'Puck'

spoon-shaped foliage, glossy and bright green... shoots of several inches carrying a number of long pale-blue bells so oddly bulging and puckered at the mouth as to resemble nothing on earth so much as a tiny soda-water bottle with a ham-frill at the end.'[3] If the botanist is unsympathetic to this description, we can only reply that it is apt and accurate.

Clarence Elliott suggested that the only answer to the slugs which find it so tempting is to grow it in such quantities that even the most gargantuan of slugs came all over bilious at the sight of the beds of it.

It obtained an AM in 1924. This is really one for the specialist alpine grower, but it is a greatly coveted plant which is not easy to keep going, especially through the winter. One of the main causes of loss is the fact that aphids take cover under the dense mats, so weakening the plant that it succumbs to any sort of subsequent onslaught. Usually, once the aphids are found it is already too late, so prophylactic action is indicated by gently applying a mild systemic spray.

Campanula zoysii in tufa crevice

References

1. John Raven, *A Botanist's Garden* (1971) p. 210
2. R. Farrer, *The English Rock Garden* (1918)
3. Ibid., p.174
4. Margery Fish, *Cottage Garden Flowers* (1961), p.40
5. Harold & Joan Bawden, *Woodland Plants and Sun-lovers* (1970), p.64
6. Geoffry Ely, *And Here is Mr Streeter* (1950), p.147
7. *Gardeners' Chronicle*, No.51 (1897), p.451
8. Ibid., No.56 (1899), p.151
9. Anon.
10. Robin Lane Fox, *Better Gardening*, p.91
11. David Stuart & James Sutherland, *Plants from the Past*, (1988), p.95
12. Fish, *Cottage Garden Flowers*, p.40
13. Fish, *Ground Cover Plants* (1964), p.46
14. Lane Fox, *Better Gardening*, p.91
15. *The Garden* (July 1901), p.58
16. Farrer, *The English Rock Garden*, p.187
17. A.E. Gairdner, 'Campanula persicifolia and its tetraploid form 'Telham Beauty',' *Journal of Genetics*, vol. xvi, no.3 (1926)
18. Alphonse de Candolle, *Monographie des Campanulées* (1830), p.313
19. Rev. Wolley Dod, *Gardeners' Chronicle* (Sept 1895), p.335
20. Gairdner, *Campanula persicifolia...* 'Telham Beauty', p.341
21. Christopher Lloyd, *The Well Tempered Garden*, p.84
22. Tassel, *Gardeners' Chronicle* (1845), p.224
23. Farrer, *The English Rock Garden*, p.193
24. *Gardeners' Chronicle* (Nov 1901), p.328
25. *The Garden* (1918), p.129
26. Farrer, *The English Rock Garden*, p.193
27. William Sutherland, *Handbook of Hardy Herbs and Alpine Flowers*, p.182
28. Lane Fox, *Better Gardening*, p.92
29. E. K. Balls, *Gardeners' Chronicle* (Apr 1938) p.283
30. Farrer, *The English Rock Garden* , p.199
31. Ibid, pp. 205-206

APPENDIX
SOCIETIES AND SOURCES OF SEED

UK SOCIETIES

Alpine Garden Society
The Secretary, AGS Centre, Avon Bank, Pershore, Worcestershire, WR10 3JP, UK

Cottage Garden Society
The Membership Secretary, Hurstfield House (CGS), 244 Eddleston Road, Crewe, Cheshire, CW2 7EJ, UK

Hardy Plant Society
Administrator, Mrs Pam Adams, Little Orchard, Great Comberton, Nr. Pershore, Worcs, WR10 3DP, UK

National Council for Conservation of Plants and Gardens (NCCPG)
The Pines, Wisley Garden, Woking, Surrey, GU 23 6QB, UK
There are National Collections of Campanulas in E. Yorkshire, Shropshire and Cambridgeshire.

Royal Horticultural Society
PO Box 313, 80 Vincent Square, London SW1P 2PE, UK

Scottish Rock Garden Club
Membership Secretary, 1 Hillcrest Road, Bearsden, Glasgow, G61 2EB, Scotland.

SOCIETIES IN NORTH AMERICA

North-West Perennial Alliance
P.O.Box 45574, Seattle, 98145 U.S.A.

Alpine Garden Club of B.C.
C/o Frank Dorsey, 4410 Ranger Avenue, N. Vancouver, BC, Canada

North America Rock Garden Society
Executive Secretary, PO Box 67, Millwood, NY 10546, USA

OTHER SEED SOURCES

RHS Plant Finder
Dorling Kindersley, 9 Henrietta Street, London WC2E 8PS, UK

The Seed Search
Karen Platt, 37 Melbourn Road, Crookes, Sheffield S10 1NR, UK.

PPP Index
Eugen Ulmer, Wollgrasweg 41, 70599 Stuttgart (Hohenheim), Germany

Seedlist Handbook
Timber Press, 9999 Wilshire, Portland, Oregon 97225 USA.
B T Batsford, 583 Fulham Road, London SW6 7BY, UK

There are also *International Plant Finders* published in Canada, Germany, Italy, Netherlands, United Kingdom and USA.

GLOSSARY

ALTERNATE	-	leaves attaching to the stem singly (not in pairs).
AMPLEXICAUL	-	the manner in which a sessile leaf clasps the stem; uncommon in *Campanula*
ANTHER	-	pollen-bearing part of a stamen.
ANTHESIS	-	time of flowering.
APPENDAGE	-	growths in the gaps between the calyx lobes.
AXIL	-	the angle between a branch or leaf and the stem which gives rise to them; generally the upper one, in which a bud often originates.
AXIS	-	(imaginary) line running through the centre of an organ.
BASAL	-	the leaves at soil level.
BRACT	-	a much-reduced leaf at the base of a flower.
CALCIPHILE	-	lime-loving; or at least growing on limestone.
CALCIPHOBE	-	lime-hating; growing on acid soils.
CAPSULE	-	a dry fruit, or seed-case, which splits to shed seed.
CALYX	-	outer whorl of flower; in *Campanula*, made up of five sepals or calyx lobes (and with or without appendages, according to species).
CAMPANULATE	-	bell shaped; in our genus, opposed to infundibular, rotate or tubular.
CARPEL	-	stigma, style and ovary as a total structure.
CAULINE	-	pertaining to, or borne on, the stem and above ground level, generally referring to leaves.
CLONE	-	a plant produced from another single plant by vegetative propagation; members of a clone all have identical genetic make-up.
CORDATE	-	heart-shaped; correctly referring to the leaf base, but frequently to the whole leaf.
COROLLA	-	the whole whorl of petals.
CRENATE	-	rounded marginal teeth of leaf.
CRENULATE	-	diminutive of previous.
CYMOSE	-	inflorescence or flower-cluster with each side stem ending in a single flower, opening successively from the tip.
DECIDUOUS	-	dropping off at end of season; as opposed to evergreen.

DECUMBENT	-	prostrate (of stems) but with ascending tips.
DEHISCENCE	-	splitting open when mature (anthers, capsule, etc.).
DENTATE	-	teeth of leaf-margin directed radially outward.
DENTICULATE	-	diminutive of foregoing.
DISTAL	-	remote from the attachment, as opposed to proximal.
ENDEMIC	-	growing only in a given area.
ENTIRE	-	(leaf) without teeth at margin.
ERECT	-	upright carriage (usually of capsule); opposed to pendent.
EXSERTED	-	(style) projecting beyond the tips of the corolla.
FLEXUOUS	-	(leaf or stem) wavy.
GLABROUS	-	smooth; without hairs, spines, etc.
HERBACEOUS	-	not woody.
INCLUDED	-	not projecting; shorter than corolla.
INFLORESCENCE	-	whole flower-cluster.
INFUDIBULAR	-	funnel-shaped, where the flower is not bell-shaped, nor the petals reflexed.
LANCEOLATE	-	lance-shaped.
LAMINA	-	(leaf) blade.
LINEAR	-	long, narrow, with parallel margins.
LOBE	-	(corolla or calyx) the individual segment.
LYRATE	-	a multi-lobed leaf with the rounded terminal lobe much larger than the side lobes.
MARGIN	-	(leaf) edge.
MONOCARPIC	-	flowering only once, dying subsequently.
MULE	-	a vernacular term describing a non-fertile hybrid, just as a mule is the infertile progeny of a horse and a donkey.
OBLONG	-	rectangular with rounded corners.
OBOVATE	-	egg-shaped, with narrower end nearest stem, two-dimensionally.
ORBICULAR	-	flat and circular in outline.
OVATE	-	egg-shaped with the wider part nearest stem, two-dimensionally.
OVOID	-	egg-shaped, three-dimensionally.
OVULE	-	seed before fertilisation.
PANICLE	-	repeatedly branched inflorescence.
PEDICEL	-	flower-stalk.
PERIANTH	-	petals + sepals, collectively.
PETIOLE	-	leaf-stalk.
PORES	-	small openings (generally in leaf surface).
PROSTRATE	-	lying flat on ground.

PROXIMAL	-	nearest to point of attachment
PUBESCENT	-	hairy as a general term.
RACEME	-	single flowers attached to the stem by a pedicel.
REFLEXED	-	bent downward or backward, usually abruptly.
RHIZOME	-	prostrate underground stem, tending to root and throw up stems at the nodes.
ROSETTE	-	cluster of leaves at ground-level.
ROTATE	-	wheel-shaped; flat, circular corolla; in *Campanula* often star-shaped.
SCABROUS	-	surface roughened by wart-like growths.
SEPAL	-	lobe, or segment, of calyx.
SERRATE	-	(leaf) having sharp forward-facing teeth.
SESSILE	-	(leaf) without a footstalk.
SINUS	-	cleft between lobes of petals or sepals.
SPIKE	-	single flowers attached directly to the stem.
STAMEN	-	male reproductive organ of a flower; the filament bears the anther, the pollen-producing part
STELLATE	-	star-shaped.
STIGMA	-	part of style receptive to pollen
STOLON	-	slender modified stem which runs along the ground, often rooting at the nodes, as in the strawberry.
STYLE	-	the long upgrowth from the carpel, the tips of which are the stigmas (usually in threes or fives in campanula).
SUB	-	prefix meaning 'almost'.
TAXON	-	any named botanical category (eg. genus, species, variety, form, cultivar).
TRIFID	-	(style) split into three parts.
TUBULAR	-	in campanula it refers to the flower shape which is a long tube-shaped bell, often with flaring tips to the petals.
TYPE	-	the originally described plant to which the given name has been attached.
TYPE LOCALITY	-	the place from which a given plant was described.
UNDULATE	-	wavy.
WHORL	-	ring of organs.
WINGED	-	usually refers to the leaf-stalk which is not round but is flanged along its length, the effect being of a narrow downward continuation of the leaf surface (as in the primrose).

BIBLIOGRAPHY

Bacon, L., *Alpines,* Newton Abbott, 1973

Bailey, L.H.,. *A Garden of Bellflowers,* New York, 1953

Beddome, Col, R.H., 'An Annotated List of the Species of Campanula', *RHS Journal,* 1907

Blamey, M., & C. Grey-Wilson, *The Illustrated Flora of Britain & Northern Europe,* London, 1989

    Mediterranean Wild Flowers, London, 1993

Bloom, A., *Hardy Perennials,* London, 1957

    Perennials for Trouble-Free Gardening, London, 1960

    Alpines for Trouble-Free Gardening, London, 1960

    Hardy Perennials, London, 1991

Boissier, E., *Flora Orientalis,* Vol 3, Geneva, 1875

Bowles, E.A., *My Garden in Summer,* London, 1914 and revisions

Clapham, Tutin & Moore, *Flora of the British Isles,* Cambridge, 1987

    Campanulas and Bellflowers in Cultivation, London, 1959

Crook Clifford H., 'Campanulas: Their Cultivation & Classification', *Country Life,* 1951

Correvon, H., 'The Genus Campanula', *The Garden,* 1901

Davis, PH, *Flora of Turkey and the East Aegean Islands,* Vol 6, Edinburgh, 1978

de Candolle, A., *Monographie des Campanulées,* Paris, 1830

de Candolle, A.P., *Sistematis Naturalis Regni Vegetabilis, Pars 7: Campanulaceae,* Paris, 1839

Erhardt, A. & W., *PPP Index,* Stuttgart, London, 1919

Farrer, R., *The English Rock Garden,* London, 1919

    My Rock Garden, London, 1920

Fitter, A. & F., & M. Blamey, *Wild Flowers of Britain & N Europe,* London 1978 and revisions

Fournier, P., *Les Quatre Fleurs de France,* Paris, 1977

Gray, Asa, *Synoptical Flora of North America, Vol II,* Part 1, New York, 1987

Greuter et al, *Med-Checklist,* Vol 3, 1980

Griffith, Anna N., *Collins Guide to Alpines,* London, 1964

Griffiths, M., *Index of Garden Plants,* London 1964

Harkness, M., *The Seedlist Handbook,* London, 1993 and revisions

Heath, R.E., *Collectors' Alpines* London, 1981

Hills L.D., *The Propagation of Alpines,* London, 1959

Huxley, A., *Mountain Flowers in Colour,* London, 1967 and revisions

    & Taylor,W., *Flowers of Greece and the Aegean,* London, 1977

ed., *The New RHS Dictionary of Gardening,* London, 1994

Ingwersen, W., *Manual of Alpine Plants,* Eastbourne, 1978

Kohlein, F., *Enziane und Glockenblume,* Stuttgart, 1986

Landolt, E., & K.M. Urbanska, *Our Alpine Flora,* Zurich 1989

Mabberley, D.J., *The Plant Book,* Cambridge, 1996

Perry, F., *Collins Guide to Border Plants,* London, 1957

Polunin, O., *Flowers of Europe, A Field Guide,* London, 1969

    Flowers of Greece and the Balkans, Oxford, 1980

    & Smythies B.E., *Flowers of South-West Europe,* Oxford, 1973

    & Stainton, A., *Flowers of the Himalaya,* Oxford, 1984

Prichard, M., 'The Genus Campanula', *RHS Journal,* 1902

Rasetti, F., *I Fiori delle Alpi,* Rome, 1980

RHS, *The RHS Plant Finder,* London, Annual edition

Robinson, W., *English Flower Garden,* London, 1883 and revisions

Roemer and Schultz, *Systema Vegetabilium*, 1819

Schauer, Th., Caspari C., *Flore et Faune des Alpes* , Paris 1973

Shishkin, B.K., *Flora of the USSR*, English translation by the Israel Program for Scientific Translations, Jerusalem, 1972

Sibthorp & Smith, *Prodromus Florae Graecae*, 1806

Tutin, TG, et al, *Flora Europaea*, Vol 4, Cambridge, 1976

von Bieberstein, FA, Marschall, *Flora Taurico-Caucasico*, 1808-1818

INDEX